D0263864

WALKING THROUGH SCOTLAND

WALKING THROUGH
SCOTLAND

DAVID & KATHLEEN MACINNES

Published in collaboration with
The Ramblers' Association

DAVID & CHARLES
Newton Abbot   London

HUNTER PUBLISHING
New Jersey

We dedicate this book to our children.
Their faith in it and in us was greater than our own.

British Library Cataloguing in Publication Data

MacInnes, David
    Walking through Scotland.
    1. Walking   2. Scotland—Description
    and travel—1981- —Guide-books
    I. Title   II. MacInnes, Kathleen
    914.11'04858   DA870

    ISBN 0–7153–9045–7 (UK)
          1–55650–003–3 (USA)

© David & Kathleen MacInnes 1981, 1987
First published, 1984
Revised paperback edition, 1987

All rights reserved. No part of this
publication may be reproduced, stored
in a retrieval system, or transmitted,
in any form or by any means, electronic,
mechanical, photocopying, recording or
otherwise, without the prior permission
of David & Charles publishers plc

Printed in Great Britain
by Redwood Burn Ltd   Trowbridge   Wiltshire
for David & Charles Publishers plc
Brunel House   Newton Abbot   Devon

Published in the United States of America
by Hunter Publishing Inc
300 Raritan Center Parkway   Edison   New Jersey 08818
Tel: 201 225 1900

CONTENTS

FOREWORD

Until the appearance of this book by David and Kathleen MacInnes, there had been no publication of any size on walking in Scotland as a whole. Books on mountaineering in Scotland abound, but not on rambling. This distinction has been fully appreciated by the MacInnes', who offer walks that are challenging but not daunting or dangerous – in other words, walks that can be undertaken comfortably by a fit person of almost any age. They have paid close attention also to such things as overnight accommodation and the availability of public transport – the happy result being that the walker can dispense with car, tent and sleeping bag.

For all these reasons and more, The Ramblers' Association is very pleased to be associated with this book. It is the third book published by David & Charles in collaboration with The Ramblers' Association and we like to think that – thoroughly researched and attractively presented as it is – it matches the high standard set by the other two.

Alan Mattingly
Secretary, The Ramblers' Association
August 1980

ACKNOWLEDGEMENTS

We would like, first, to acknowledge the multitude of our forebears who trod out or built the many paths and tracks now so delightful to tramp; and the Scottish people for their forbearance in leaving large tracts of magnificent scenery to the sheep, the deer, the grouse and the walker.

Second, we have had help from many people in Scotland: in walking some of the routes, in advising and vetting our material and in sharing our enthusiasm. M. Fearn of Edinburgh trod some of the Argyll Walk with us and for us. H. Ralph of Motherwell assisted on a number of the Walks. S. Hetherington of Boat of Garten, President of the Strathspey Mountaineering Club and peripatetic walker, did the whole Strathspey Walk for us and tried, unsuccessfully, to raise our day's mileage limit to match his tirelessness. J. Fladmark, of the Countryside Commission, provided extensive advice and encouragement. Members of the Scottish Tourist Board, The Highlands and Islands Development Board, the tourism departments of the Regions and many local tourist organisations were unstinting in their help. And D. G. Moir of Edinburgh, whom we met only in the pages of his excellent though laconic compendium *Scottish Hill Tracks*, directed us to many of our recent walks. T. and K. Flynn of Edinburgh helped by doing a number of Walks (they having the misfortune of being related to the authors). I. MacInnes, the only child over whom we still have some control because of age, walked, criticised profoundly, ran errands and did research as well as bearing the burden of a disrupted household while the book was in process.

On the far side of the Atlantic our American friends have rallied notably. L. Hull did the Carrick Walk (in street shoes, no less). G. and D. Foust spent two weeks in Scotland as the deadline neared, helping us walk and record data in Mull, Breadalbane and the Southern Uplands. K. Prusso advised on route-finding techniques. J. Clymer was our researcher on things Scottish. J. Rice, our typist, went far beyond her task in her interest and encouragement.

Last but foremost was the help of our editor, Pam Darlaston of David & Charles. Her labour with our 'mid-Atlantic' prose was notable, her letters to us models of lucidity, encouragement and, on occasion, restraint.

Finally, you may ask – with all that help – what were we, the authors, responsible for? The mistakes, of course, and most of the fun.

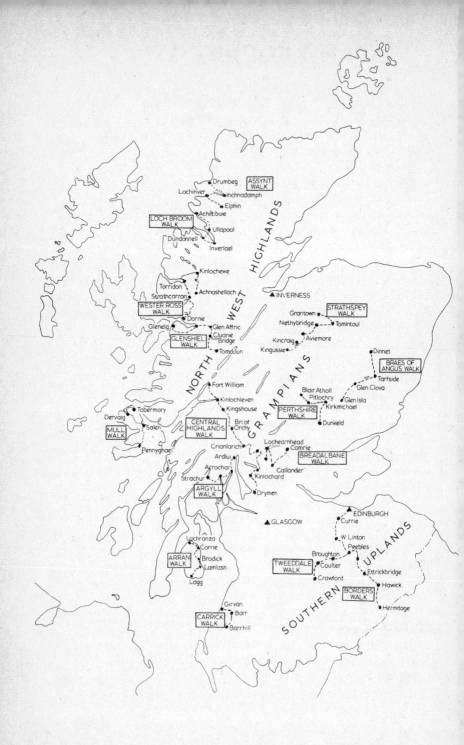

INTRODUCTION

Scotland is unique in possessing wild but easily accessible uplands of great natural beauty. You can take a walking holiday through these hills, enjoying their peace and solitude, yet coming at the end of each day to a night's lodging offering comfort, catering and sociability. Moreover, because Scotland has reasonable public transport, these walks can be easily started or completed by train or bus, obviating the difficulties in linking a car to such journeys. This book brings under one cover the essential information to make such walking holidays technically and aesthetically satisfying.

We have always felt that walking is the best way to see and appreciate Scotland. There is a big difference between 'taking a walk' from your car or lodging and embarking on a walking journey of several days' duration. Our aim is to offer this pleasure to those who have never experienced it as well as to provide a useful guide for those seasoned walkers who presently hesitate to embark on 20- to 25-mile walks carrying heavy packs, eating out of tins and sleeping in the rain. Instead we offer walks lasting a number of days, with a limit of 10 to 15 miles per day, and with accommodation and public transport available along the way. We provide information on each of our Walks which should enable you to arrange walking tours tailored to your interests and capabilities. The tedious and time-consuming task of gathering the necessary information on how to obtain transport and accommodation is done for you. Because each section (a day's walk) can be reached or left by public transport, you have great flexibility in arranging a walk to fit the length of your holiday. Indeed, although the book is written for those who want an extended holiday away from modern transport, all the sections, except those taking you into Glen Affric and Kirkmichael, can be done as single-day excursions.

The book is therefore a working guide which, when used with the suggested Ordnance Survey maps, should enable you to find and walk each track with a minimum of path-finding. The Scottish hills are generally bare, however, and many of these tracks are little used, therefore the way is not always clearly defined and the walker is occasionally on his own. This will not bother the experienced rambler but may perhaps upset the less experienced. We try to offset this problem by providing careful path data at critical points and by a separate section on Route Finding (see page 172), an addition we have not found in other guidebooks.

Using the book

There are 15 Walks each of 2 to 8 days' length giving a total of 59 days' walking covering 700 miles (1130km). The 15 Walks are grouped into four upland areas; the Southern Uplands, the Grampians (East and Central Highlands), the Northwest Highlands and the Islands. For ease of identification, the Walks are named after their local area (Carrick Walk, Assynt Walk, for example). Each of the Walks is introduced on two or four pages. The first page contains a map and a listing of the sections (single-day walks). Distances are given as well as information on public transport and accommodation (for an explanation of the notations on these latter, see Public Transport and Accommodation, page 168). The succeeding pages contain a general description of the Walk and of its overnight points. We can only point a finger at the riches each Walk offers; you may wish to explore further for yourself through the varied literature available (see Further Reading, page 186). The walks are arranged in one direction of travel (Hermitage to Edinburgh in the Borders Walk, for example) but may, of course, be done in either direction.

The introductory map (page 8) shows the locations of all the walks. Some of these lie in close proximity to each other and it is possible, with a little ingenuity, to use sections from different walks to make your own combination walk (the easiest place to do this is with the Borders and Tweeddale Walks, for example, as they share a common overnight point).

Each day's walk (section) is contained on two facing pages for ease of use (a feature we have seen in no other guidebook). These two pages include a brief overall description of the walk, detailed path-finding information and a sketch or two. The sketches are to help you visualise what you may see on the walk in a way that words alone cannot.

The heading of each day's walk gives the two overnight points, the distances and elevations gained (the differences between the lowest and highest points) and the Ordnance Survey maps needed. The distances and elevations will help you judge how strenuous the walk may be and how long it should take. The map numbers refer to the Ordnance Survey 1:50,000 series (1¼in/mile). While the heading gives the distance and elevation in both English and metric units, within the text distances are given in miles and elevations in metres. This is a compromise in order not to burden the reader with two sets of numbers everywhere. We chose the mile measurement because it remains the more understandable distance unit and metre because it is the unit used for elevations in the 1:50,000 series maps. The spelling of place names is taken from these maps and you may blame the Ordnance Survey if you feel that violence has been done to the Gaelic spelling.

Other Walks

We have by no means exhausted the possible walking tours in Scotland. We have selected, within the criteria of distance, accommodation and public transport, tours in every upland area of Scotland, giving a wide range of scenery and walking difficulty. Other tours can be made up and we suggest D. G. Moir's *Scottish Hill Tracks, Vol 1 & 2* as the best source, which lists some 250 walks of 5 to 35 miles' length. Even this number does not exhaust the possibilities – a cursory look at any 1:50,000 series map will show many others. The publications of the Scottish Tourist Board and the Scottish Mountaineering Trust listed in Further Reading on page 186, and W. A. Poucher's *Scottish Peaks* detail many others.

BORDERS WALK S. Uplands
82½ miles (133km)

SECTION	DISTANCE	OVERNIGHT POINTS
1	14½m (23km)	Hermitage-Hawick
2	12m (19km)	Hawick-Ettrickbridge
3	10½m (17km)	Ettrickbridge-Innerleithen
4	12m (19km)	Innerleithen-Peebles
5	13½m (22km)	Peebles-West Linton
6	13m (21km)	West Linton-Currie
7	7m (11km)	Currie-Edinburgh

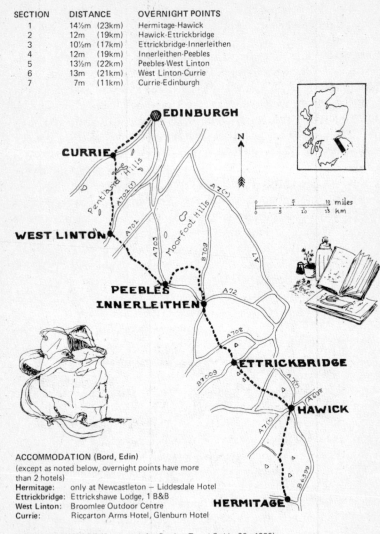

ACCOMMODATION (Bord, Edin)
(except as noted below, overnight points have more
than 2 hotels)
Hermitage: only at Newcastleton — Liddesdale Hotel
Ettrickbridge: Ettrickshawe Lodge, 1 B&B
West Linton: Broomlee Outdoor Centre
Currie: Riccarton Arms Hotel, Glenburn Hotel

PUBLIC TRANSPORT (Bord — ask for *Borders Travel Guide*, 30p 1980)
Hermitage: bus Newcastleton or Hawick, bus Hawick-Edinburgh, bus Newcastleton-Carlisle
Hawick. bus Edinburgh or Carlisle
Ettrickbridge: bus Selkirk, bus Selkirk-Edinburgh
Innerleithen } bus, Glasgow or Edinburgh
Peebles
West Linton: bus Peebles, Glasgow or Edinburgh
Currie: bus Edinburgh
Edinburgh: major transport centre

One of our two long routes, the way passes by old drove roads and hill tracks, from the English-Scottish border through the heart of the southern uplands to the city of Edinburgh. The country is wild enough to satisfy most walkers' tastes but has charming Borders towns and villages in which to spend the night. It is sheep country, the very names of some of the geographic features – Cheviot Hills, River Tweed – telling as surely as the woolly animals on the hills what was and is a major industry here. In walking, there is the counterpoise between the remote solitude of grass, bracken and heather-clad uplands and the pleasant woods and farms of the river valleys.

OVERNIGHT POINTS – **Hermitage** has a small cluster of houses and, a mile away in the desolation of the moors, a great grim double-towered castle. The castle is open to the public. **Hawick** is the largest of the Borders textile towns. The points of interest are: St Mary's Church, consecrated in 1214 and rebuilt in 1763; Mote Hill, the mound of a Norman castle; Wilton Lodge, a museum housing a collection of Borders relics; and the Horse Monument. The Monument recalls the defeat of English marauders in 1514 by local youths, the town's grown men having been nearly wiped out at Flodden a year earlier. **Ettrickbridge** is a tiny village which takes its name from an old bridge over the Ettrick Water. The bridge was rebuilt in 1777. **Innerleithen**, on the River Tweed, once a popular watering spa, is now known for its knitwear and tweed. One mile south is Traquair House, one of the oldest inhabited houses in Scotland (open to the public). It dates from at least 1209 when William the Lion held court there. **Peebles** (see Tweeddale Walk). **West Linton,** a village at the foot of the Pentland Hills, was once the meeting place of drovers. In earlier times it was known for its stonemasons and an example of their work may be seen in Lady Gifford's Well. It has been designated a conservation area and the village is much restored, with charming nooks and crannies to explore. **Currie** is a village on the Water of Leith, with paper mills an important industry. **Edinburgh** is dominated by its great castle high on a rock above the city and by Arthur's Seat (200m). Below the castle are the Princes Street gardens, a glory of colour in season, and Princes Street itself, renowned for its shops. High Street, or the Royal Mile, descends from the castle past medieval tenements to the Palace of Holyrood House. To the west of the castle is the eighteenth-century Georgian 'new town.'

1 HERMITAGE–HAWICK
14½miles (23km) 1130ft (345m) OS 79

Certainly Hermitage Castle is a fitting start or end for our Borders Walk. Not only does it feature in typical Borders history, with its ownership violently changing between Scotland and England, but also, more romantically, it was the scene of the clandestine visit by Mary Queen of Scots to the bedside of her wounded lover, Bothwell. This impulsive act nearly cost her her life and certainly damaged her reputation.

The isolated site adds to the mood of this imposing structure but it also adds to the problem of using it as a starting or ending point. Nearby accommodation is nearly non-existent (some unlisted farm B&Bs). You must stay in Newcastleton (5 miles south) and take the morning bus up, if starting at Hermitage, or the afternoon bus down if finishing there. You could try writing to the Postmaster at Hermitage for local B&B information. In spite of these minor problems, we include this walk for those intrepid romantics who will take the time and trouble to overcome these difficulties.

The walk itself is a challenging and beautiful one, through a lonely, sparsely settled area of steep, rounded hills and deep, narrow ravines. Modern man's mark is noticeable by his reafforestation and by his grazing animals, but the farms are few and scattered along the even scarcer farm roads. There are no villages or towns and the main roads lie many miles away from the walk.

Ancient man has also made his mark and you should look out for the Tinlee standing stones, seen at a distance as you approach Dod. Forts and settlements are just north of Dod and are particularly visible from the Dod farm road. The site was being excavated by archaeologists when we passed.

Do not be misled by the seeming ease of the route on the OS map. It is largely trackless between Braidliehope Farm and Dod and the forest shown as only on the eastern flank of Hawk Hill has now been extended down its side and over on to Dod Rig, adding to the confusion and rough footing. It is not too difficult, however, but just requires careful attention to map and compass as well as where you place your feet. The footing is poor to excellent.

NORTH – From Hermitage take the castle road up Hermitage Water from the B6399. In ¾ mile you will pass the castle and in 2½ miles on the R, a farm road going R crosses Hermitage Water and goes past Braidlie Farm to Old Braidlie. The latter is a fine stone house which has now become a cattle byre, its windows broken and its doors

14

down. Follow the track up the E side of Queen's Mire but when it veers W leave it and go trackless up to the rise of land just E of the top of Swire Knowe. You should look for a gate in the fence here and go down a small wet ravine to a forest road. As you walk down this road towards the building shown at the foot of Dod Rig, you will see a green ride in a newly planted forest on the opposite slope through which you will shortly pass. Continue down until just before the road joins another road and here take the ride you have just seen. Go uphill to the fence at the edge of the plantation and pick up a track going N. This will carry you through Dod Farm to a narrow paved road. Hawick is 6 miles to the N.

SOUTH – Take the secondary road S out of Hawick towards St Leonard's Park and Pilmuir (ask locally if in doubt). While climbing up this road and still in the town, you will pass a small clock tower in the middle of the road and thus know you are proceeding correctly. In 6 miles you will come to Dod (not to be confused with Dodburn, which you pass first). Go through the farmyard, keeping straight ahead on a track. You will soon come to a newly planted forest. Cross the fence on your R and follow it down to a forest road at a fork. Take the R fork and go S uphill until the road ends. From here follow a small burn up Swire Knowe, coming at the top to a gate. Go through this gate and continue S down Swire Knowe and along the E slope of Queen's Mire to the farm road past Old Braidlie and on to a paved road. Go L 2½ miles to Hermitage and the B6399.

Hermitage Castle

2 HAWICK–ETTRICKBRIDGE
12 miles (19km) 1540ft (470m) OS 73 & 79

This is a fairly easy walk, over high moor and farmland, between the great wool town of Hawick on the River Teviot and the quiet valley of Ettrick Water. At Ettrickbridge a farmer invited us to watch the sheepshearing. We were impressed with what a back-breaking job it is, literally. The man shearing must perform the task in a bent-over position, with the protesting sheep's head held firmly between his knees. It takes an amazingly short time for an experienced shearer to shear each animal. Two younger men were at work with electric clippers while an incredibly old-looking man was using old-fashioned hand shears; he was only seconds behind the younger ones at his task. Our young son helped the farmer's son roll up and load the fleece into the wagon. As they did so, this young Borders lad gave us a short lesson on sheep.

First he identified for us three of the main breeds we had been looking at. Those who have roundish white rubber-like muzzles (ghost faces) are Cheviots, their lambs being like stuffed toys with rose-petal pink ear linings and noses. The Border Leicesters also have white faces. Their faces are flatter and less smooth, their ears are longer and lie forward rather than sideways. The sheep seen the most everywhere in Scotland are the Scots Blackface. Both the ewes and the rams have horns, and their faces are almost perpendicular and are spotted black and white. We also learned about the different wool characteristics. Blackface wool is coarser and tougher than Cheviot wool and is used for carpets and tweed rather than for finer material. Different breeds even have different grazing habits. The Blackface graze separately while Cheviots graze as a flock, therefore the latter need pastures where grass replaces itself more quickly so you do not see them up north. Our final piece of information was that sheep are more destructive to a pasture than cattle, the reason being that cattle munch only a couple of inches off the top of herbiage, leaving the roots undisturbed, whereas a sheep pokes its muzzle further down and often damages the roots.

The walk has sweeping views of the Teviot and Ettrick valleys and the hills beyond. It is a mild challenge in path-finding but crosses safe country with civilisation hidden but close at hand. The small task of finding your way together with the constantly changing scenery makes it a fine part of a walking holiday. However, if the high ground is enveloped in mist, only experienced walkers should venture across. The footing is good to excellent.

NORTH – From the W bridge over the Teviot in Hawick, go N round the town car park and take the Wilton Park Road L. In ¾ mile, a little beyond the sign to the Wilton Park Museum, go R on to the Whitehaugh Road. Follow this road to the end of the paving at Whitehaughmoor Farm (2½ miles). Here take the farm road R which turns and runs NW out to the open moorland. On the moor pick up a track running W and then NW across the top of the moor to a paved road coming in from Shielswood (5¼ miles). It is easy to lose this track and just using your compass will have you climbing a number of fences, some electrified. The best solution is to work your way by the gates which lie across your general direction of travel. The next gate will usually be in sight from the one you are passing. You will skirt a small plantation on your L, ½ mile off the track, near your first gate and shortly after you will see far ahead a dip in the skyline through which you will pass just short of a paved road. Shielswood Loch is not seen until you near the road. Once at the road, the way to Todrig is visible to the NW. Leave the road and cross the steep little valley of Ale Water (fording the Water anywhere) and walk up to the E side of a long wall going N along the W slope of Leap Hill. Here you will pick up a track which will carry you to a paved road beyond the Todrig Burn. Go L (W) on this road to Todrig and Langhope, go through the Langhope Farm yard (signs here 'To Loch') and take a track NW across the moors past Akermoor Loch (the track passes closer to the loch than the map shows) to the foot of Helmburn Hill (the NW edge of the plantation on Caver's Hill runs parallel to the track about ½ mile W of it). You can go either way around Helmburn Hill but the W way is shorter. Both tracks come down to the B7009 E of Ettrickbridge. The B&B accommodation is just across the bridge and Ettrickshawes Hotel is 1¼ miles W on the B7009.

SOUTH – Walk E on the B7009 and cross the bridge over Ettrick Water to the first farm road on the R. This will lead you around the W side of Helmburn Hill. Beyond, take the **NORTH** directions in reverse.

cheviot

blackface

3 ETTRICKBRIDGE–INNERLEITHEN
10½ miles (17km) 980ft (300m) OS 73

Yarrow Kirk

The joy of this walk is that it includes two of the most attractive glens in the Borders, Ettrick and Yarrow. The surrounding hills are not high but they are bare, with mantles of heather and bracken. These contrast sharply with the sinuous pattern of verdant grass, trees and shrubs which the rivers provide on the valley floors. The climb up and down Witchie Knowe by road still has a wildness about it even though the surface is now paved. A digression to explore the old Kirkhope Tower is almost irresistible. The little village of Yarrow offers lichen-covered stone buildings and walls set off by many bright flowers. There is also old Yarrow Kirk to visit. This is still an active church, whose ministers often serve for very long periods (53 years was the longest). When standing inside the Kirk, it is easy to envisage it filled with its congregation of long ago which included both human and canine shepherds. Reputedly, when the human members rose to sing the benediction at the end of the service, the dogs joined in enthusiastically. The canny minister finally solved the problem by not having their masters rise!

After the intervening bleak section north of the Yarrow Hills, the sight of green Traquair Valley and the Strath of the Tweed beyond is a welcome one. You pass by the pedestrian entrance to Traquair House which, if you are not too tired, is worth a visit.

NORTH – Go W from Ettrickbridge on the B7009 for 1 mile to the paved road over Witchie Knowe (370m) (locally called the Swire). If you want to visit Kirkhope Tower take the road just W of the bridge, go out past a cemetery and strike across country 1 mile to the grim old fortified house. From here walk W across to the Swire ½ mile away. At the top of Witchie Knowe there are good views back into the

18

Ettrick Valley and ahead to the Yarrow Valley and the hills beyond. The road runs down along the E side of Rough Knowe and comes out on the A708 at Yarrow. The Kirk is just across the road and is worth a visit. Go R on the A708 for ¼ mile to a gate on the L, which is just beside the gate and road to Deuchar Farm. After going through the gate, pass along the fence to a track which goes up the E side of the burn and over the saddle between Glengaber Hill and Peatshank Head. An attractive alternative is to climb up Deuchar Hill and follow the cairns along its ridge to the same point. When crossing the saddle make for a gate in a long E–W stone wall. Here the track goes N towards the forested top of Black Rig. Although it is not shown on the map, this track continues on to Black Rig. There is no track down to Glengaber Farm (a white building) past which you wish to go, so leave the track and head directly for the farm by the easiest way. Once there you go N on an LRT. This takes you down to Damhead Farm and the B709, 8¾ miles from Ettrickbridge. Innerleithen is 1¾ miles to the R.

SOUTH – From Innerleithen walk S on the B709 through Traquair to the Damhead Farm road (1¾ miles). Go through the gate and turn R through the farmyard, keeping the house on your L. Go uphill on an LRT past a young forest on your R. The LRT goes along the side of the hill, with Fingland Burn, the farm road and the forested hill in the near distance on your L. When the LRT forks, keep L and you will soon come to the white building of Glengaber. Head E on a track which soon disappears and continue uphill on that heading until you strike a N–S track going along the ridge of land. Go S on this track to a gate in a long stone wall that runs E–W. After going through this gate the track continues S down a steep narrow valley to the A708. In clear weather you can get much better views by going L along the top of Deuchar Hill (cairned) and down. Go R on the A708 to a narrow paved road running L over Witchie Knowe to the B7009 in Ettrick Valley. Ettrickbridge is to the L.

still in use

4 INNERLEITHEN–PEEBLES
12 miles (19km) 1100ft (335m) OS 73

Craighope

This is a leg-stretching walk, by forests and moors, from Innerleithen to Peebles, both wool towns on the Tweed. There is enough solitude to give a strong sense of isolation but with civilisation close enough for a feeling of safety. The landscape shows the full range of reafforestation, from seedlings in newly furrowed ground, through mature forests, to felled areas. It also shows the pleasing visual effect of austere sweeps of heather giving way to the more gentle cloak of forest green. The footing is generally good, the way fairly easy to find.

WEST – From Innerleithen walk a few hundred yards on the A72 and then go N on the B709 in the valley of Leithen Water. At 1¼ miles from Innerleithen, just before a river bridge (there is a fish weir here), turn L up a farm track that swings parallel to the river but in sheep pasture high above it. Below, the river snakes through the fertile green valley, with the opposite hills crowned by new forest. Continue straight ahead past a farm building and skirt a small forest on your R into pastures again, where the track going N peters out. Here you must pick your own way across country parallel to the B709 below. Your goal is the road that turns NW off the B709 and follows the Leithen Water through a ravine. To reach this road you will have to cross the river on a very narrow footbridge. (Caution: when making your way across country towards this road, be careful not to choose a contour too high on the hillside because if you do you will encounter steep ups and downs as well as dense heather as you near the ravine.) Once over the bridge, go L on the road, past Leithen Lodge, through a flat, rather dull valley with new forest plantings and several houses, to a gate and a forest road. Care must be taken to avoid branching roads here – your heading is W. You will finally come to Craighope, a large empty croft. Beyond Craighope the forest road forks. Take the L fork, which doubles back and seems to be heading in the wrong direction. However this is just a switchback of the steep way up the S side of the narrow ravine made by the burn flowing down to Craighope. This road ends abruptly at the head of the ravine. Climb steeply up the most northerly of several grassy ways to the top of the ridge, rather like climbing a wall made of a down quilt. From the top you will see another forest road 100yd ahead, with a fork in view. Just at this fork there is an indistinct double track going SW at right angles to the furrows of a newly planted forest. Take this track through an old stone wall to a well-defined path going R, down the S side of Makeness Kipps (in clear weather there is a radio tower in view from here – keep it well to your L). Peebles will now come into sight. The path leads down through a forest, crossing several forest roads, to the grass-covered ruins of Shieldgreen Tower, with long views across the Tweed valley. Beyond the ruins, the path descends steeply to a cottage and the forest road which goes down to the A72, joining it just to the E of the Hydro Hotel. Peebles is ½ mile to the R.

EAST – Walk ½ mile E on the A72 out of Peebles, to a narrow paved road going N along the E side of the Hydro Hotel. It turns into a forest road which climbs steeply to the ruins of Shieldgreen Tower. Here a path goes NE along the S slope of Makeness Kipps. When it turns abruptly towards the radio tower on Dunslair Heights, leave it and head across new forest, crossing a road that goes along the ridge. Go directly E across heather and bracken to a steep ravine. A forest road high on the S side of the ravine is reached by negotiating the steep grassy slopes at the head of the ravine. This road descends to a large empty croft at Craighope, from which a forest road goes out past Leithen Lodge to the B709. Innerleithen is 3½ miles to the R (S) on this road.

larch

5 PEEBLES–WEST LINTON
13½ miles (22km) 590ft (180m) OS 72 & 73

Kidston

This is an easy walk over fertile green hills and through a forest plantation, from the Borders town of Peebles on the Tweed to the village of
West Linton on Lyne Water at the edge of the Pentland Hills. There
are broad views of the Tweed valley to the south and the Lyne valley
and the Pentlands to the north and west. The way is easy to find, the
footing fair to excellent. As we walked along the farm road beside
White Meldon Hill we were intrigued by the number of whimbrel
which flew over and around us, their long beaks making them look
like miniature curlews.

If you stay overnight in Peebles, you can visit the imposing
Neidpath Castle which is situated ½ mile west of the town on the
A72, just at the edge of the River Tweed. Originally owned by the
Hays of Yester, the castle has passed through various hands and is now
owned by the Earl of Wemyss and March. It fell into disuse in the
seventeenth century and gradually decayed until work commenced on
its recent restoration. Its construction was begun in the fourteenth
century and it has been added to and rebuilt over the centuries. It now
lacks its battlements and is a curious mixture of habitable fort and
fortified house. Its known military history is limited, but it was
garrisoned against Montrose in 1645 and against Cromwell's forces in
1650. It is an L-shaped tower on a rocky outcrop rising some 80ft
above the river. Although it appears conventional on the outside, the
inside is a hotch-potch from frequent rebuilding and it is a challenge to
sort out the changes. It is worth puzzling over.

NORTHWEST – Go W on the A72 from Peebles town centre and
take the first R after the A72 makes a sharp R and L. Go N for ¾ mile

to Standalane Farm where a sign points uphill to a public footpath to the Meldon Hills via Hamilton Hill. The way climbs up a grassy track between two fences, with beautiful views of the pasture lands and hills beyond. You soon come out in the open on a path which circles halfway round Hamilton Hill. Ignore a path which forks R and continue round until you see Upper Kidston Farm with its narrow strip of forest. Ignore the path through the farm shown on the map and make for the NE corner of this strip of forest. A track skirts the wood to a narrow paved road going N. Take this road and, at its junction with another road going towards Wormiston (these roads have almost no traffic), turn R to the first farm road on your L (to Stewarton Farm) (5 miles from Peebles). Go W on this road for ½ mile to a N–S rough track and go N and then W to the farm buildings at 461217. Beyond, the track enters a plantation on a wide forest ride and goes W over a gentle rise to a broad new forest road at Greenside (7 miles). Go L on this road to its end and then continue directly ahead on a pathless, somewhat boggy ride that carries you through to a gate on the open moorland below Wide Hope Shank. From here go N along the forest edge, cross Flemington Burn and go up Green Knowe to the *second* of two farm tracks. Go L on this track which will carry you up the valley of the Fingland Burn (good views of Lyne Valley at the top) and down to the A701 at Damside (10½ miles). Go R ½ mile to the B7059, then L to West Linton.

SOUTHEAST – Damside is not marked but is a farm road just opposite a small wooden bus shelter. Go straight uphill on a rough farm track. At Flemington Burn leave this track, cross to the forest edge and go S to the first gate. Beyond, screened by a single line of trees, there is a ride going uphill. Push through the trees and follow the ride up and then L across the slope to a new forest road. Just beyond the second side road leading L down to the Greenside clearing, a track goes R uphill, leading to Stewarton. When you reach the paved road beyond Stewarton, go R and then L towards Upper Kidston. Follow this road to the first L turn (farm road to Nether Kidston) and take it until you meet on your R the path going up SE to join the public footpath that goes round the E side of Hamilton Hill on down past Standalane Farm to the road leading to Peebles.

oak

6 WEST LINTON–CURRIE
13 miles (21km) 935ft (285m) OS 65

go under

This walk carries you over the Pentland Hills, a long stretch of handsome uplands that runs south from the edge of Edinburgh. The area is a favourable haunt of walkers, a nearby haven from the busy city streets. The local authorities, who over the years have steadfastly refused to permit housing and industrial developments here, are to be fervently thanked. Coming north, you pass through open upland like much of that you will have already crossed on your walking holiday; but coming from Edinburgh, with all its city charms, into this open countryside is like meeting a good friend after a long absence. The hills have long been inhabited, the earliest evidence being hut circles, those faint rings slightly greener than the surrounding grass. The hills are mostly grazing land, as well as a catchment area for Edinburgh's water supply. Thus you pass numerous reservoirs, with sheep on the surrounding slopes. Many of the hills are over 500m in height and the walk gives wide views of the Lothian Plain to the north and the Lammermuir Hills to the southeast.

The walk goes along the eastern edge of the Pentlands by way of an old Roman road then by a hill track across the hills past West Kip (550m) to Bavelaw Castle and by country roads and paths to Currie on the Water of Leith. The way is easily followed, the footing being poor to excellent.

NORTH – In West Linton take the track heading off the A702 W uphill opposite the B7059 junction. Follow this to a narrow paved road and turn R (N). At 1¼ miles from West Linton the paved road goes L to Baddingsgill House but a track, marked 'the old road' on early maps, runs straight on N from a signpost 'Carlops 1¾ miles; public footpath'. This 'old road', said to be Roman, leads down to the A702 just S of Carlops. About ½ mile before Carlops the track runs through a 'village' of summer chalets and caravans. Not a caravan park at all, much more pleasing to the eye – little chalets and ancient

24

go through

caravans nestling in niches or topping rises, an example of how loving use over a prolonged period tends to bring man's artifacts into harmony with the environment. (Carlops is a corruption of Carline's Leap, a carline being a witch). Go N on the A702 through Carlops, then ⅛ mile past the bridge over the River North Esk, take a steep track off to the L to a narrow paved road. Go R to Nine Mile Burn. From here a track signposted 'Balerno by Broadlaw' continues ahead through a gate. At the next gate turn L (NW) and follow a stone wall up the hill to another signpost. This directs you N on a track which winds up to a saddle between Braid Law and Cap Law and passes around the N side of Cap Law and the SW side of West Kip (6½ miles). The track goes down and across Kitchen Moss, a broad valley, and passes W of Hare Hill to a stile by a gravel road. Go R on the road a short distance to the Bavelaw Castle estate road (8½ miles). Go L on the estate road, down through a line of trees and past the Threipmuir Reservoir. ¼ mile beyond the reservoir turn R on a track which leads you to a path along the NW side of the reservoir. Beyond the reservoir the path turns L to a narrow road at Harlaw Farm. Go R on this road to Middle Kinleith. Here a path goes downhill beside a wooded burn and strikes another paved road just by the Glenburn Hotel. If not stopping at the Glenburn Hotel, at the crossroads between Wester and Middle Kinleith, go L ¾ mile to Currie. The Riccarton Arms Hotel is on the A70 near where you enter the town.

SOUTH – follow the **NORTH** directions in reverse.

go over

7 CURRIE–EDINBURGH
7 miles (11km) 160ft (50m) OS 66

Although this is a short, easy ramble, the walk is interesting as it goes by an abandoned railway along the Water of Leith and along the towpath of the old Union Canal into the heart of Edinburgh. Appropriately, it ends in the medieval part of Edinburgh at the gates of the imposing Edinburgh Castle, from whose high ramparts the whole city can be surveyed and the temptations of the shops and restaurants be contemplated. This is a unique experience, to come by quiet byways into the centre of a busy city. You follow the deep wooded valley of the Water of Leith, crowded with the history of the early Industrial Revolution, going back to the late fourteenth century. Before the coming of the steam engine the Water provided the motive power for as many as 71 mills. The walk then goes by the old canal, and through city streets to the castle. Not only is it a walk through 600 years of history but the way is well wooded and, through Colinton Dell, as charming as any in Britain.

NORTH – In Currie, walk E down Kirkgate Road from the A70 and cross Currie Brig, reputed to be 600 years old. Just over the bridge, take the steps down to the footpath beside the abandoned Balerno branch rly. The rly, opened in 1874 in response to the growing needs of the mills along the river, operated its last trains in the late 1950s when many of the mills were closing. The sharp curves of the line on this branch necessitated the use of special four-wheeled wagons. For the next 3¾ miles you will be walking in the valley of the Water of Leith, which is filled with trees, shrubs and other flowering plants (the Scottish Wildlife Trust has recorded 147 different plant species). It is also lined with old mills, a few still operating. The earliest recorded date concerning a mill is 1376. As you walk N, the first burn coming in from the R is the Poet's Burn in the Poet's Glen (so named for James Thomson, a contemporary of Robert Burns). When the path goes under Blinkbonny Road (the first bridge you pass) the outflow of the lade is all that remains of a snuff mill that operated from 1749 to 1920. You shortly cross the river and pass one of the few still active mills, opened in 1792. At Juniper Green you will go under a bridge and pass a weir and an archway of a mill lade, the last evidence of the Juniper Green Corn Mill. Next, before coming to a road which goes out of the valley, is the Woodhall Corn Mill which has been operating since 1704. Farther on, at a point where a footpath goes L out of the valley, the Upper Spylaw Mill still stands, one of the earliest mills (1590). Its top floor was once an inn, a resort of smugglers. You soon pass Spylaw Park on the R, with its fine residence, Spylaw House (1650), now used by a Scout group. The path passes through a long tunnel and enters Colinton Dell. You can continue by the rly path but the way is prettier if you go R to the footpath along the river following it until the third footbridge where, just before the bridge, you take a path L back to the rly. The rly path soon crosses the canal and you take the towpath R. The canal was opened in 1822 to bring coal to Edinburgh and operated until 1963. It runs for 32 miles joining the Forth–Clyde canal at Falkirk and, in its heyday, provided a comfortable overnight passenger service to Glasgow. You will pass no locks but you will walk over a long aqueduct passing high above the Water of Leith and the village of Slateford (now a part of Edinburgh). The towpath has been given a fine surface and it is an easy stroll. The way leads at first past playing fields and suburban gardens but gradually the city houses and factories rise on either hand. When you reach a lift bridge where a crossing road is level with the towpath (you can see the end of the canal 100yd ahead) go L to Fountainbridge Road, but before you do, depending on the time of year, look for nesting swans in the long grass across the canal. Go R on Fountainbridge Road, cross Lothian Road to Bread Street and go on to the Grassmarket below the castle. Follow the signs to the castle and your journey is over.

SOUTH – Walk S down North Wynd Street, a set of steps off High Street, 200yd E of the Edinburgh Castle gates, to the Grassmarket. Go W on Bread Street to Fountainbridge Road and continue to Gilmore Place, the first street after the Bingo Hall. Go L a few yards to the canal then R along the towpath for 2 miles to bridges going over both the canal and the street beyond. Cross these bridges to a footpath along an abandoned rly and follow this path for 3¾ miles to Currie.

TWEEDDALE WALK S. Uplands
33 miles (53km)

SECTION	DISTANCE		OVERNIGHT POINTS
1	13½m	(22km)	Peebles-Broughton
2	7m	(11km)	Broughton-Coulter
3	12½m	(20km)	Coulter-Crawford

ACCOMMODATION (Bord)
Peebles: more than 2 hotels
Broughton: Greenmantle Hotel, 1 B&B (Kilbucho House)
Coulter: Hartree Hotel (2m), 1 B&B (Ladyholm),
              B&Bs at Causewayend (1¾m)
Crawford: Crawford Arms Hotel, Lindsay Tower Hotel

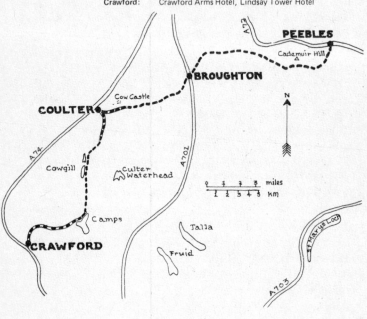

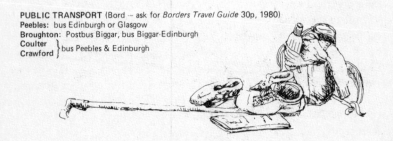

PUBLIC TRANSPORT (Bord — ask for *Borders Travel Guide* 30p, 1980)
Peebles: bus Edinburgh or Glasgow
Broughton: Postbus Biggar, bus Biggar-Edinburgh
Coulter ⎱ bus Peebles & Edinburgh
Crawford ⎰

The Tweeddale is not considered part of the Borders, as the people we met on the Walk so vehemently told us. But politicians, ever oblivious to such distinctions, called it Peeblesshire and Peebles is definitely a Borders town, as the town people also told us. The history of the area is equally as turbulent as that of the Borders. It is marked by the remains of many hill forts and defended settlements, now faint earth-works or piles of stones on hilltops, and by its numerous ruined castles. Today it is peacefully rural, with the only martial voices those of the shepherds controlling their dogs. It is an important sheep-breeding area but cultivated fields patchwork the valleys below the sheep-filled hills and cattle are also much in evidence.

The Walk explores the variety of scenery that Tweeddale has to offer. It passes through farmland and upland pastures, crosses inhabited river valleys and climbs high on moors. It uses quiet country roads, farm tracks and old hill tracks as it threads its way west and south from the Tweed to the upper reaches of the Clyde. The area was heavily populated by ancient man and the Walk passes the remains of their defended habitations, a delight to amateur antiquarians. It is not strenuous, the elevations gained are modest but the views are superb. At the end of the day you will have the feeling of having done a ramble well worth the effort. The overnight points are small, quiet villages except for the active town of Peebles.

OVERNIGHT POINTS – **Peebles** is a royal burgh on the River Tweed, noted for its tweed mills. The town has a spacious High Street with an old Mercat Cross. The ruined Cross Kirk, standing high on the bank of a burn running through the town, was founded by Alexander III in 1261. There is a museum in the Chambers Institute, housed in the oldest part of a building called the Dean's House. Its collection is chiefly from the local area and includes archaeology, social history, wildlife and geology. The fine parish church at the end of the High Street was built in 1784. Among the town's hotels two are notably old, the seventeenth-century Cross Keys and the early nineteenth-century Tontine. The fifteenth-century Neidpath Castle, ½ mile to the west, is open to the public. **Broughton** is a small village on Biggar Water. Beside its ruined church is a restored vault, said to be the remains of a cell occupied by the seventh-century Pictish St Lludan. There are traces of several hill forts and settlements nearby. **Coulter** is an equally small village, in a farmland setting. **Crawford** is a village in the upper Clyde valley on a byway off the main road. Just outside is Tower Lindsay, a fragment of an old castle. A section of a Roman road runs on the other side of the river.

1 PEEBLES–BROUGHTON
13½ miles (22km) 620ft (190m) OS 72 & 73

This is a walk of great scenic variety, from the busy Borders town of Peebles on the River Tweed to the tiny village of Broughton on Biggar Water. The route passes over a hill sprinkled with the remains of Iron Age forts, crosses two heather-clad ridges by way of old hill tracks and wanders along a tree-girt stream. There are constantly changing views of hills, valleys and farmland. The way is generally easy to find. The hill tracks are obscure in places but go by well-marked valleys and along burns so it would be difficult to get lost. The footing is poor to excellent.

WEST – From the centre of Peebles walk S on the B7062 across the bridge over the Tweed. Bear R when the B7062 goes L and take the second L (Edderston Road). Continue up to Tantah and go through a gate on to a faint track which follows the walls of Tantah. Follow this track until it becomes more pronounced, leaves the walls of Tantah and goes SW round the plantation. When you approach the end of the plantation at the point where a settlement is noted just R of the track, you can leave it and climb Cademuir Hill (no track) to walk along its ridge. The views are superb from the ridge in all directions and you can explore the fort sites noted on the map. Come down off the ridge at its SW end by striking directly for Hallyards across a smooth, grassy slope. The hill is a bit of a climb and a steep descent but the effort is most rewarding. However, if the weather is poor or you prefer the easier way, keep to the track which goes W of the plantation and joins a paved road going W and N round the base of the hill. At Weirs turn L to the Glack (5 miles). Just beyond a sharp bend in the road a farm track starts R between two buildings and goes W beside a burn. The track and burn soon peter out but it is a simple matter to continue W to the top of the ridge ahead and descend W with a plantation on your R to pick up a farm road going down past Easter Dawyck Farm to the paved road at Stobo Kirk (7¼ miles). Go N 200yd to a farm road (Easterknowe Farm), passing by the kirk (worth a short walk to view). Go up the farm road for another 200yd to a track going L along Easter Burn. Follow this track for a delightful 1½ miles to Harrowhope Farm. It is lined in part with great oaks and beeches and by gnarled Caledon pines, affording an unusual experience in Scotland. Beyond Harrowhope Farm the track climbs NW and W to the S ridge of Mid Hill (a R fork before the ridge top is to be ignored). There is a fort and settlement several hundred yards above and to the L of the two small forests ahead, but keen eyes are needed in order to see much. Beyond, the track drops down and crosses the Hopehead Burn and an LRT (10¼ miles). Beyond the LRT the heather hides the old track and it is best to head W up the E shoulder of Hammer Head and across its N slope (the track becomes evident in places here) to a gate in the pass between Hammer Head and Broomy Side. From the gate, head SW down to the Hollows Burn and pick up a faint track going S near the W side of the burn. This track, becoming increasingly clear, will carry you to Broughton Place (a handsome late Scots Baronial building now an art gallery). Go down its access road to the A701. The Greenmantle Hotel is 300yd to the L.

EAST – From the Greenmantle Hotel in Broughton go N on the A701 for 300yd to a road going R to Broughton Place. Take this road, passing a large house and farm building beyond, to a track going N up the valley of Hollows Burn. At the head of the valley the map shows the track joining another coming E from Stirkfield. This can be found but is so faint as to be useless. Therefore it is better to strike E from the head of the burn and you will soon see the gate leading into the Hopehead valley. From the gate you will see a faint track running along the N slope of Hammer Head to its E shoulder. Once on the shoulder, the track beyond, up the W side of Mid Hill, can be clearly seen across the valley. Go down the heather to this track, over Mid Hill and down to Harrowhope Farm and a farm road to Stobo Kirk. From here go through Easter Dawyck Farm and ascend to the ridge on the S side of a plantation and down across the fields to the Glack. Go L on a paved road to the first paved road R and out past Weirs to a track going E round the base of Cademuir Hill to Peebles.

keep your distance

2 BROUGHTON–COULTER
7 miles (11km) 375ft (115m) OS 72

faithful shepherd

This is a short easy stroll along quiet country roads and sheep-filled valleys. Its major attractions are the remains of Iron Age settlements and forts that crown the hills along the way. The easiest to reach is Cow Castle, a ring of defensive walls circling the top of a steep grassy hill a few yards north of the walk. Since the basic walk is easy, you may wish to explore these ancient monuments. The high ridge of White Hill (399m) on the north side of the walk has two forts and there are two more near Cow Castle. It is a friendly relaxed place. As we ate our lunch by the side of the road, a horsewoman stopped to chat. Newly returned to her home from abroad, her enthusiasm for the delights of Tweeddale was contagious and her friendly sharing of valley life rewarding to us. Further on our way, a patient car driver sat while a herd of sheep slowly ate their way along the grass of the verge towards an open gate. As we chatted with him, we thought of the impatient city drivers fretting a few moments at a red light.

WEST – Leave the Greenmantle Hotel in Broughton and walk S on the A701. Just across the bridge over the Biggar Water go W on a narrow paved road. Follow this road for 3 miles to a farm road going sharp L to Mitchell Hill Farm (not marked). Take this road and go through the farmyard to a track going W through a broad valley. The ruined Kilbucho Church is downhill across a burn. There is a small cemetery attached and the place is worth a visit. Follow the track as it goes along the N side of the valley until you pass a large stone-walled field. Leave the track here and cross the valley to its S side, picking up an older track that carries you through the valley to Nisbet Farm. ¾ mile before the farm, the track passes between hills some 100m in

32

height, with Iron Age forts. The hill to the N contains Cow Castle, the remnants of two successive fortifications. There are three concentric walls, each with an external ditch, the outer wall and the ditch being the earlier. Because the local stone is too broken to lend itself to wall-building, the walls were probably turf crowned by closely set posts. Traces of timber-framed houses were found within the walls. There is a smaller fort on the same hill 200yd away to the NE, a single wall and ditch being in evidence. The hill to the SE, less than 400yd distant, has a similar fort. If these forts were built and occupied at the same time, one wonders at the relationship between them. They could hardly have been hostile towards each other as food-raising would have had to be done jointly on the land below. It seems likely that the forts would have been built sequentially as the population expanded. However, a determined enemy would find it possible to defeat the group piecemeal. You can do your own speculating.

At Nisbet Farm follow its farm road to a narrow paved road going NW to Coulter. The single B&B (Ladyholm) is ¼ mile N of the Post Office, L off the A702. The Hartree Hotel can be reached by going N on the A702 to the first crossroads and following their signs R. More pleasantly, take the road NE just before the Culter Allers House, past the church and turning off L at East Mains, going past Legholmshiels and Thriepland to the road to the hotel (follow the OS map). The hotel is 2 miles from Coulter. There are several B&Bs on the A702 at Causewayend, S of Biggar, 1¾ miles from Coulter.

EAST – Go SE from Coulter on the road to Birthwood and in ½ mile go L to Nisbet Farm and through the farmyard to a track going NE. In a few yards take a R fork up to and past Cow Castle. Follow this track E to Mitchell Hill Farm and a road going E to Broughton.

rowan

3 COULTER–CRAWFORD
12½ miles (20km) 1565ft (477m) OS 72

This is a more strenuous walk than the amble to Coulter from Broughton but is similar – the beginning and ending sections are on deserted country roads in quiet green valleys and the middle section is a track over a high hill. There is an interesting trackless bit up a steep ravine to a notched pass then down another valley followed by a walk along the shores of a reservoir. The way is easy to follow, the footing fair to excellent. One of the interesting things about this walk is the wildlife that is visible above 300m. Because the walk is relatively easy you will have ample opportunity to survey your surroundings. You will be startled by the profusion of life about you. Scotland's birds of prey, for instance, although relatively few, may be seen here by those with keen eyesight. The golden eagle, 'king of the Scottish skies', haunts high passes (such as the one between Windgate Bank and Hudderstone). It is now usually found further north but other birds of prey such as hawks and falcons frequent the same type of terrain. One of the things that enables the uplands to support a relatively large population of raptors is a profusion of rabbits. Warrens abound everywhere in this region and the density of rabbits may be as much as 50 per acre. You can hardly walk this area without seeing a dozen rabbits. You might also spot a hare of which there are two types in Scotland; the common hare (brown coat) which lives in the valleys and lowlands, and the blue mountain hare (grey-blue coat) which is slightly smaller and lives upwards of 300m. The mountain hares turn white in winter.

SOUTH – Leave the A702 in Coulter just at the sharp bend before the bridge over Kilbucho Burn and go S on the road to Birthwood. In 1¾ miles, shortly after the Culter Allers Farm, take the R fork marked 'To Cowgill Reservoirs'. At 3 miles a track goes L, taking you straight up and over Cowgill Rig to the head of Cowgill Upper

Reservoir. Leave the track when it reaches the floor of the Windgate valley and go SE past ruins up and through a notch between Windgate Bank and Hudderstone. Beyond the notch follow the E bank of the Linn Burn down to an LRT along the Grains Burn, 6¼ miles from Coulter. There is no track other than those made by sheep between Windgate and the Grains Burn but it would be virtually impossible to get lost since you follow the narrow Windgate valley up and the Linn Burn down. Go R on the LRT to the head of Camps Reservoir and take a narrow paved road running along the W side of the water. At the foot of the reservoir cross the dam and go out the reservoir access road to Crawford. On this latter section there is a henge through which the road cuts, 100yd before the turnoff for Normangill Farm (a henge is a circular bank with an inner ditch, probably used for religious ceremonies, and dating back to the second or third millennium BC. A few henges, most notably Stonehenge, have stone circles associated with them). At Midlock the remains of a Roman road go SE along the E bank of the River Clyde but it is not distinguishable from the average farm track. As you pass Crawford Farm you will see a ruined castle, Tower Lindsay, to your L. It is worth inspecting (at a safe distance, since it is in the last stages of decay).

NORTH – Use the **SOUTH** directions in reverse. When coming up the LRT along the Grains Burn, Linn Burn is just opposite the edge of the plantation shown on the OS map. The pass into Windgate Valley will not be seen until you are well up Linn Burn. Beyond the pass the most easily followed route is to go down to the valley floor to the track going up over Cowgill Rig. However, lazy but able walkers can save 200m in climbing Cowgill Rig by going from the pass along sheep tracks through the heather following the 500m contour on the E slope of Hudderstone and meeting the track further along.

CARRICK WALK S. Uplands
18½ miles (30km)

SECTION	DISTANCE		OVERNIGHT POINTS
1	7½m	(12km)	Girvan-Barr
2	11m	(18km)	Barr-Barrhill

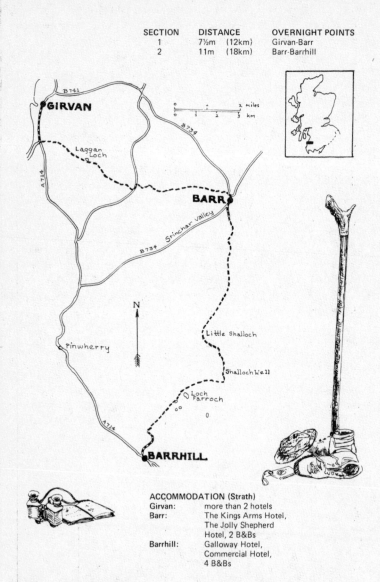

ACCOMMODATION (Strath)
Girvan: more than 2 hotels
Barr: The Kings Arms Hotel,
             The Jolly Shepherd
             Hotel, 2 B&Bs
Barrhill: Galloway Hotel,
             Commercial Hotel,
             4 B&Bs

PUBLIC TRANSPORT (WSMT-bus)
Girvan: bus or train Glasgow, Prestwick & Stranraer (ferry Stranraer-Ireland)
Barr: bus Girvan
Barrhill: bus or train Glasgow & Girvan (rly station ¾m from town centre)

An easy Walk across the peaceful and lonely open Carrick uplands. It is ideal as a two-day 'starter' for more strenuous and difficult Walks or as a lovely beginning or end to a visit to Scotland. The Carrick area, (the name is derived from the Gaelic word for rock) is a land long populated, attested to equally by its ruined castles, hill forts and burial cairns and by its fertile valleys. There are wide views of pastured hills and rolling moorland to 300m elevation, and, near Girvan, a sweep of the Irish Sea. Ten miles offshore lies Ailsa Craig, a high island (348m). This is a unique feature of the seascape in this area. It is sometimes possible to make arrangements with a local boatman to visit the island, depending on weather and tides. Like its counterpart Bass Rock on the east coast, it is a breeding ground for gannets but it also has a lighthouse and a ruined castle. It is often called 'Paddy's Milestone' as it is halfway between Glasgow and Belfast. The lively tourist town of Girvan and the charming villages of Barr and Barrhill are overnight points. The route is easily accessible from Glasgow, Prestwick Airport and Stranraer (ferry to Ireland). Short lengths of the Walk are pathless, affording a mild introduction to compass and map work.

OVERNIGHT POINTS – Barr is an interesting village of about 150 inhabitants. It lies at the confluence of the Stinchar River and the Water of Greg some 7 miles east of Girvan. The village is set in a high valley among hills and is a well-known salmon-fishing centre. At the edge of town on the B734 is a fine bridge over the Stinchar, dating from 1787, with a single arch and humped roadway. A number of white-washed eighteenth-century cottages, set in rows typical of the period, have been restored. The village is a conservation area, the intention being to maintain the charm of the eighteenth-century architecture. **Barrhill,** in the Duisk valley, is a somewhat larger village than Barr and is a centre for fishing and shooting. **Girvan,** situated on the Ayrshire coast, is a pleasant seaside holiday resort where once King Robert the Bruce held his courts. Initially it was mainly a fishing village but it has grown through tourism and the addition of a few industries. The harbour and waterfront are attractive, the shops numerous, the sandy beaches excellent for swimming, and fishing is available on the Water of Girvan. If you stay over, there are also many short walks in the neighbourhood. Within a 3-mile limit are both Killochan Castle (c.1586) and the sixteenth-century Ardmillan House where Mary Queen of Scots once stayed.

1 GIRVAN–BARR
7½ miles (12km) 950ft (290m) OS 76

A pleasant walk across rolling upland pastures filled with sheep and cattle. There are wide views below of Girvan and the Irish Sea, with Ailsa Craig, a volcanic core island, about 10 miles offshore. Curious and playful young steers may run towards you, and follow along, intimidating the city person, but their shape is quite different from the bulky and irascible mature bull who needs a field to himself. Laggan Loch, now difficult to find, has a legend that the outline of a ploughman, complete with yoke, can be seen on the surface of the water. He is reputed to have been lost in the mud at the bottom of the loch. The track is faint to nonexistent in places and rough compass headings need to be followed. You will pass a few typical upland farms and farm buildings. The footing is fair to good.

Girvan

EAST – At the roundabout connecting the A77 and A714 1 mile S of Girvan (harbour), turn due E on a macadam road. At the first bend, bear R onto a narrow dirt road. Cross a rly and climb through woods on to pastureland. There are ruins of an Iron Age fort on Dow Hill ¼ mile S of the track about ½ mile past the rly. The track grows faint and disappears at 2½ miles, near Laggan Loch. Although no farm buildings are visible from the loch, there are remains of a small shack and boat. At 4 miles cross the Pinmore–Penkill road and pass a large quarry. From here find your way E across pastureland to Barr. Just before Barr the River Stinchar may be encountered if you come S of Barr. There are bridges at Barr and at Auchensoul Farm 1 mile S of Barr on the B734 road. The river can be forded if not in spate.

and WHO are you?

WEST – Go N on B734, across the River Stinchar. In ¼ mile turn W uphill between two burns on a faint track which peters out. Continue across trackless moorland on a W heading to cross the Pinmore–Penkill road at Tormitchell in 4 miles. Go W and then NW across pastureland past Laggan Loch to a farm road coming up from Glendoune, over a rly to the A714 1 mile S of Girvan.

2 BARR–BARRHILL
11 miles (18km) 750ft (230m) OS 76

Barr

Similar to the Girvan–Barr section, but longer and with a slightly confusing forest to negotiate, this section offers open views across rolling pastures and moors. We were feeling especially in tune with our surroundings on the morning we set out on this section because of our experience the evening before at the pub in Barr. It was one of those rare instances when we were privileged to get an intimate glimpse of a different life. We began the evening sitting with a 75-year-old retired professional fiddler who spouted A. E. Housman to us through his umpteenth beer. With him was a young fiddler from Glasgow who regaled us all with his genuine talent. He loved to play and was able to give any tune asked for and we all asked until midnight. The convivial mood he set drew forth lots of local lore from three brothers who joined us. One, a shepherd, told us much about sheep and shepherding, interspersing his remarks with many a long passage from Robbie Burns recited as it ought to be. Somehow it seemed to be just what we should be doing on an evening in a little village in Scotland – a fitting prelude to our day's tramp.

SOUTH – Go S on the B734 out of Barr for ½ mile to Alton Albany Farm. At the farm turn S on a farm road, signposted 'Public Footpath by Black Clauchrie to Barrhill 11'. Go up road, which leads past White Knowes Farm at 1½ miles. It becomes a track which gradually grows fainter until it disappears. The turnoff to Black Clauchrie at 2 miles is not visible. You will take the direction to Little Shalloch, moving S and then SW along the slope of Greensides, crossing Muck Water at 3 miles. Just beyond the ruins of Little Shalloch, skirt the edge of a forest to the first ride (a wide treeless swath). Follow the ride until the forest track from Mark is met, turning SE and then S on the track to Shalloch Well, then either (a) S to Balmalloch, W to White Fell Plantation and SW to Balluskie and Barrhill, or (b) S and W around the forest and SW past Loch Farroch to Knocky Skeaggy Loch and SW along the NW edge of a forest to a farm road, SE to Balluskie and on to Barrhill. The forest just beyond Little Shalloch is confusing and if you feel you have lost the way, head SW on any convenient ride to get clear of the forest and, once in the open, go S to pick up the path or SSW to hit Loch Farroch, then SW to a plantation ½ mile beyond Loch Farroch. If unable to find these points, head S or SW and in about 3½ miles from Little Shalloch some farm road will be picked up and directions to Barrhill can be obtained from the first farmhouse.

NORTH – From the centre of Barrhill, walk NW to a bowling green on your R, then turn N on a farm road to a fork ¼ mile N of Balluskie, go NW for ½ mile to the first curve, then strike NE off the road uphill along the plantation on your L, then another plantation on the R, to Knocky Skeaggy Loch and Loch Farroch. From Loch Farroch head NE for the S end of a large plantation about 1 mile away, and N through a forest past Shalloch Well to Little Shalloch. If unable to find your way in the forest, go out the E edge of the forest and N along the W slopes of Arecleoch Forest, Pindonan Craigs and Greensides until Muck Water is crossed, then head N to White Knowes Farm and the farm road leading to Alton Albany Farm and the B734 just S of Barr.

CENTRAL HIGHLANDS WALK
Grampians 94 miles (150½km)

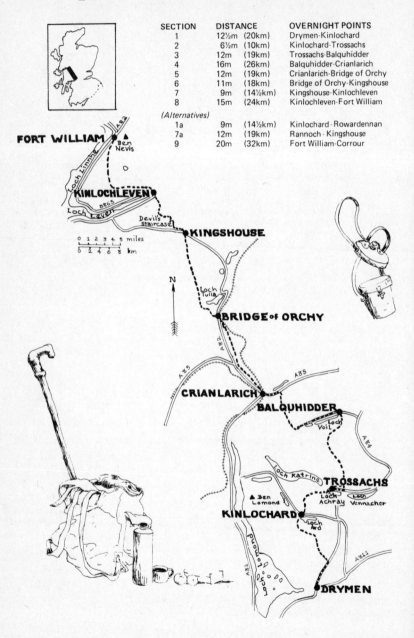

SECTION	DISTANCE		OVERNIGHT POINTS
1	12½m	(20km)	Drymen-Kinlochard
2	6½m	(10km)	Kinlochard-Trossachs
3	12m	(19km)	Trossachs-Balquhidder
4	16m	(26km)	Balquhidder-Crianlarich
5	12m	(19km)	Crianlarich-Bridge of Orchy
6	11m	(18km)	Bridge of Orchy-Kingshouse
7	9m	(14½km)	Kingshouse-Kinlochleven
8	15m	(24km)	Kinlochleven-Fort William
(Alternatives)			
1a	9m	(14½km)	Kinlochard - Rowardennan
7a	12m	(19km)	Rannoch - Kingshouse
9	20m	(32km)	Fort William-Corrour

ACCOMMODATION (Cent, Ft Will for Fort William and Kinlochleven)

(except as noted below, overnight points have more than 2 hotels)

Kinlochard:	Forest Hills Hotel, Altkeith Hotel, Maples B&B
Trossachs:	Trossachs Hotel, Loch Achray Hotel, several B&Bs at Brig o' Turk (2 miles)
Balquhidder:	Ledcreich Hotel, Stronvar Guest House
Bridge of Orchy:	Bridge of Orchy Hotel, Inveroran Hotel (2 miles)
Kingshouse:	Kingshouse Hotel only
Kinlochleven:	B&Bs

(Alternatives)

Rannoch:	Rannoch Moor Hotel only
Corrour:	Youth Hostel only (1 mile)
Rowardennan:	Rowardennan Hotel, Youth Hostel

PUBLIC TRANSPORT (H&I)

Drymen: bus Glasgow (Buchanan Station)
Kinlochard: postbus Aberfoyle (Mon-Sat), bus Aberfoyle-Glasgow (Buchanan Station)
Trossachs: bus Stirling, train Stirling-Edinburgh/Glasgow
Balquhidder: as above from A84 2 miles away
Crianlarich
Bridge of Orchy } train or bus Glasgow (Mon-Sat)
Fort William
Kingshouse: bus Glasgow
Kinlochleven: bus Fort William (Mon-Sat)

(Alternatives)

Rannoch
Corrour } train Glasgow (Mon-Sat)
Rowardennan: boat & train Glasgow (summer only)

Our longest Walk runs nearly a hundred miles, from just outside Glasgow to Fort William and the beginning of the Great Glen. The route goes through the heart of the Central Highlands and ends at a point where public transport provides easy access to the Outer Hebrides, Skye and the North by train, bus and boat. Several famous areas – the Trossachs, Glencoe and the Fort William/Ben Nevis area are included in this walk. The way is largely through wild and scenic country, over hill tracks, and old drove and military roads. The footing is good and the pathfinding not difficult. If you walk northwards, you will move from the urbanised lowlands through the progressively more mountainous and rugged country of the Central Highlands. The Trossachs will give you a generous helping in miniature of the highlands, including a walk over a mountain peak. The walk into Crianlarich will introduce you to a high mountain pass through 1000m peaks. Glencoe has mountains massed in a bewildering profusion of buttresses, serrated ridges and soaring pinnacles. Beyond Kinlochleven lies a typical lonely mountain glen; once peopled, but now with only the sheep and the wind for company. While the Trossachs are better known to tourists, we consider Glencoe the masterpiece of the Walk. It is one of the most beautiful glens in Scotland, remembered in Scottish history as the 'Vale of Weeping' from the infamous massacre of 1692 in which a large number of the MacDonald clan were treacherously slain by Campbell soldiers, or were driven into the hills to perish from the winter cold. The surrounding hills attract climbers from all over Britain, but there are many hill paths that can be covered by the average walker. Glencoe is a rainy place and lucky is the walker who finds it in sunshine. However, a different beauty emerges when the clouds cover the peaks – dark, sombre, and menacing to some. A day of sun and clouds provide the ideal – glimpses of both sunlit and dark beauties. Nothing is more dramatic than when the clouds momentarily part to reveal a hidden peak or to allow the sun to turn the gloom into gold.

Accommodation varies greatly on this route, and ranges from the modest hospitality of pensioners' cottages in Kinlochleven to the sophisticated catering of an old inn like the Kingshouse, set in lonely grandeur at the head of Glencoe.

The route is most flexible and can be done in shorter lengths since all the sections are accessible by public transport, and there are alternative interesting sections feeding into it. One section violates the 15 mile per day rule (Balquhidder–Crianlarich, 16 miles), and another is better done by train or bus (Crianlarich–Bridge of Orchy, 12 miles) as the way runs close to the main road and the railway. There are side walks and scrambles from most of the route points (Ben Lomond from Kinlochard or Rowardennan, the hills and passes of Glencoe from Kingshouse, and Ben Nevis from Fort William, for example). The northern portion (Crianlarich–Fort William) is part of the West Highland Way, a proposed long-distance walking route from Milngavie (Glasgow) and Drymen to Fort William. We feel our southern portion offers a more interesting walk between Drymen and Crianlarich than does the West Highland Way.

OVERNIGHT POINTS – Drymen is a busy village near Glasgow, with pleasant hotels and shops. **Kinlochard** is a cluster of houses at the head of Loch Ard, a pretty loch enclosed by hills with Ben Lomond as the centrepiece to the north. The **Trossachs** or 'Bristly Country' is the richly wooded gorge of both Loch Achray and Loch Katrine; here the walker will end at Loch Achray with its two hotels and single church on the shore with Ben Venue and Ben Ann overlooking it.

Balquhidder is a scatter of houses just east of the narrow Loch Voil, which is dominatd on the north by the lofty ridge of the Braes of Balquhidder. In the graveyard of the roofless old kirk is buried Rob Roy McGregor, the famous freebooter. **Crianlarich** is a small village at the intersection of three valleys: Strathfillan, Glen Dochart and Glen Falloch. It is ringed by distant peaks, the highest being Ben More, Stobinian, Cruach Ardren and Beinn Oss. Although an ancient bridge still bestrides the River Orchy here, the **Bridge of Orchy** now consists of a hotel and railway station on the busy A81. **Kingshouse** is a lonely inn standing on the old military road in Glencoe (one of those built for the soldiers working on the roads). It is surrounded by peaks on three sides with the desolate Rannoch Moor on the fourth. **Kinlochleven** is a town built to house workers for the large aluminium plant, at the head of the fjord-like Loch Leven. It is more attractive than its industrial function implies. **Fort William** is a bustling touring centre at the head of Loch Linnhe, dominated by Ben Nevis, Britain's highest mountain. Worth visiting are the West Highland Museum and the Scottish Crafts Exhibition where one may purchase articles handmade by Scottish craftsmen.

bluebell

1 DRYMEN–KINLOCHARD
12½ miles (20km) 150ft (46m) OS 57

Loch Ard

This is one of the few walks that travel through extensive mature evergreen forests. There are 4 miles along an unfrequented road with open views of farmland, moors and distant hills, then a 7-mile stretch through sombre forests with an occasional view, and finally a descent to Loch Ard nestling under high hills. The footing is good to excellent all the way, the way is well marked and the height gained is minimal. Kinlochard is a pony-trekking centre, so on the day we walked from Drymen we were not surprised to pass a cheerful string of pony-trekkers. What did surprise us, however, was the sight of a full-grown red deer casually walking among the ponies. It was apparently a bottle-raised fawn that no doubt came to love human company and felt itself to be a pony, albeit a trifle odd in shape.

NORTH – Leave Drymen just where the A811 bends E (there is a bus stop here) and take the road N for 4¼ miles to Drymen Road Cottage. On this road you will pass through the Garadbhan Forest after about a mile. At 2½ miles the Muir Park Reservoir will be on your L, with open farmland on your R. The forest road to Kinlochard is well marked (at 4¼ miles), with a large sign a short distance off the road. You will follow the *blue* chevron posts to Loch Ard – forest road all the way, with numerous forks and crossroads. Your signpost is always just *beyond* an intersection, so you may have to sally a few yards down a wrong road to check the colour of the chevrons. At about a mile before Loch Ard you will begin to catch glimpses of the loch and the high hills beyond. As you pass around the head of the loch (W end), Ben Lomond will be glimpsed to the L. At 12½ miles the B829 will be reached, with a pleasant teashop to restore the inner person, an amenity that few walks offer. The hotels and B&Bs are to the R.

SOUTH – Go around the head of Loch Ard (W end), leaving the B829 at the teashop. Pass the Mill of Chon, now a whitewashed farmhouse. Just beyond is a tiny schoolhouse on the R and then a huddle of council houses on the L, looking out of place in that rustic setting. Past the council houses you will find a sign listing all the walks ahead, one of which is yours (this is the green-chevroned Drymen Road, 8 miles). The walks all stay together as you move around the loch head on an unpaved road (passing the Loch Ard Sailing Club, which fills the loch with white sails on a weekend). The road gradually climbs above the loch, passing scattered houses. It finally leaves sight of the loch, entering a sombre evergreen forest (especially sombre in the rain and mist). Just beyond every fork or crossroads you will find a post with paint-filled chevron slashes, denoting the way. You are following *green*. You will note on the opposite side of your posts a different colour – blue, for the northbound traveller. We assume that this is to keep you moving in the right direction even if you get completely disoriented. At about 2 miles you go under a large aqueduct and your way goes off to the L (the map does not show all the tracks through the forest. Just keep *green* in mind). There will be occasional clearings with views. The narrow paved road to Drymen will be reached at 8¼ miles with Drymen 4¼ miles to the R.

2 KINLOCHARD–TROSSACHS
6½ miles (10km) 2280ft (695m) OS 57

This is a short but fairly strenuous walk over Ben Venue (729m) with magnificent views of Ben Lomond, Lochs Ard, Katrine, Achray and Venachar and the hills to the north. At weekends it is a popular walk and you may see as many as a dozen people in a day! It is nice to eat your lunch at the top on a clear day and feast on the panorama as well as the food. The way is well marked and the footing good to excellent. Mild scrambling is needed at the summit, safe for any age. (There is a bypass around the summit of Ben Venue in case of bad weather.)

NORTH – Go up the Ledard Pony Trekking driveway, past the house and outbuildings and take the W bank of the Ledard Burn. The path is signposted *green*. The burn tumbles down through an open deciduous forest at first, with many small waterfalls – a delightful sight on a warm day. The path climbs steeply in the beginning, easing off after coming into the open. It stays high on the W side of the narrow valley of the burn for a mile, then crosses to the E bank. In another mile the path turns E along a small tributary and climbs to a col between Creag Tharsuinn and Beinn Bhreac, where Ben Venue first comes into view about a mile away. The path goes E across the N shoulder of Creag Tharsuinn, with striking views of Loch Katrine below. At 3 miles you reach a cairn from which green-marked posts go downhill to the R. You have two choices: (a) down the green-posted trail 3 miles along the Gleann Riabhach to Achray Water near the A821 (this route is not shown on the OS 57 map), or (b) directly up and over Ben Venue. For the summit route, head E uphill from the cairn (the path is intermittent), to the ridge containing the two summits. The descent to the Trossachs is from the lower SE summit. You go first due S several hundred yards down into a grassy valley. Follow this valley as it swings down and around under Ben Venue until it heads N directly towards the end of Loch Katrine. From here you drop steeply to the loch, losing some 600m in about a mile. There are only faint and occasional signs of a path but even if you stray, the way down does not lead into any danger. You will come upon a well-defined path near the loch shore running L to Goblin's Cave and R (mostly E) to the sluices and dam at the end of the loch. From the dam you can either cross to a paved road running into the regular Loch Katrine access road, or, keeping on the S bank of Achray Water, soon strike an unpaved road running down to the Loch Achray Hotel and Loch Achray itself.

SOUTH – Walk around the head of Loch Achray (W end) and up the driveway of the Loch Achray Hotel. Go R, around the back of the hotel buildings, to a forest road going uphill, when you will come upon a signpost 'To Kinlochard 6½ miles'. You have a choice of two routes from here: (a) the one marked by green chevrons, or (b) along Achray Water and Loch Katrine towards Goblin's Cave, with a faint path ¼ mile beyond the dam and sluices leading L steeply uphill to the lower E summit of Ben Venue. From here, after a rest to enjoy the view, it is best to go along the summit ridge to the higher NW summit and turn SW downhill by a track that steadily grows more visible, to a cairned saddle. Here, the signposted path (a) up the Gleann Riabhach comes up from the L. The summit route should be avoided in poor visibility or high winds as it is poorly marked and exposed. From the saddle and cairn go W along the N slope of Creag Tharsuinn to a col between it and Beinn Bhreac. Here the path turns S down the Ledard Burn to Loch Ard.

cuckoo flower

3 TROSSACHS–BALQUHIDDER
12 miles (19km) 1020ft (310m) OS 57

This walk is mostly on moorland but it includes a charming wooded two miles in the Trossachs along Loch Achray and Black Water, and a pleasant walk down Glen Buckie into Balquhidder. There are magnificent views, when on the moors, of the Strathyre Forest hills and the Braes of Balquhidder. The footing is good to excellent, the way well defined. Although there are no signs announcing the fact, you should be aware that you are now walking through 'Rob Roy country'. Rob Roy, a kinsman of the Chief of the MacGregors, lived and operated in this district as a kind of eighteenth-century Scottish Robin Hood. The romanticising of his life and exploits is such that the legendary figure is now more real than the historic one. We reread Scott's *Rob Roy* to try to capture a feeling for the man but to no avail. We hope that some day someone who speaks more clearly to contemporary readers will write another book on him. Meanwhile, we must be content to find him as and where we can in the glens through which we walk.

NORTH – From Loch Achray go E on the A821 to Brig o'Turk village. It is roughly 2 miles, pretty in the morning before the tourist traffic starts, going along Loch Achray and the meander of the Black Water. The Brig is an ancient single-arch stone bridge spanning Finglas Water. The village is just beyond – a school, a store and a straggle of houses. The turnoff (L) is not signposted but is the only road about where the map shows it. It is paved and passes by a half-dozen houses before forking. Take the R fork, signposted 'Footpath to Balquhidder 10 miles'. It rises steeply to the Finglas Reservoir, a bright sheet of water between high hills. The road, still paved, runs through a large sheep farm, finally becoming an LRT. A mile beyond, you reach a signpost to Balquhidder, directing you away from the loch (it reads '6 miles' but obviously should read '8 miles'). Still on an LRT, the way leads N up a wide valley. In about 2½ miles a third signpost to Balquhidder points the walker away from the LRT, and a series of cairns lead the way to the top of the valley and a fence. Take the R (E) of two gates and a well-marked path leads N down along another fence on to a broad flat. Here a fair-sized stream, the Calair Burn, flowing E is picked up. Follow the S bank of the burn, first just beside the water and then moving up to the high bank as the streambed deepens. Several sheep trails will serve you, and the way runs parallel with the burn to Ballimore Farm and a paved road down Glen Buckie. Go L through the Glen, past fields and plantations, through a cluster of white-washed houses at Ballinluig to the head of Loch Voil and Balquhidder, 2 miles from Ballimore Farm.

SOUTH – Just over a bridge on the road through Balquhidder from the A84 (2 miles), by a telephone kiosk, a paved road runs S. In ¼ mile a signpost to 'Brig o'Turk 10 miles' is passed. The road winds up through the woods out on to the farmland of Glen Buckie. Past Ballimore Farm just beyond a bridge over the Calair Burn a second signpost to Brig o'Turk (8 miles) takes you to the R off the road and up the S bank of the burn. Stay parallel to the burn on sheep tracks above it until a wide valley opens S. There is a well-defined path up this valley, alongside a sheep fence, with a gate through a second fence at the top (411m). Continue S down a new valley over grassy slopes. Some cairns may be encountered but there is no defined path. An LRT, coming down from the W side of the valley, will be joined at a third signpost pointing back to Balquhidder. Follow this LRT to Finglas Reservoir. It becomes a paved road down to Brig o'Turk at 10 miles. Go R on the A821 to Loch Achray.

Rob Roy

4 BALQUHIDDER–CRIANLARICH
16 miles (26km) 1200ft (365m) OS 50, 51, 56 & 57

Balquhidder

This walk violates two of our rules: it is over 15 miles and much of it is on motor roads. However, most of the latter is a quiet narrow road in a beautiful loch-filled valley. Only 2 miles are on a busy highway and even here there is a safe wide grassy verge on which to walk. The high spot is a long easy climb up and then down remote and wild valleys with mountains on either hand, gaining 365m in altitude. This stretch is trackless but the way is by burns except for less than ½ mile over a conspicuous saddle. Even in the mist there is little danger of getting lost – the most approximate compass heading will bring one over the saddle to the next burn. The footing is good to excellent. The road walking can be shortened by hiring a taxi: in going north, from Balquhidder, take the taxi (hire from Lochearnhead) for as much of the way to Inverlochlarig as you wish: and in going south, from Crianlarich, for the 2 miles to Benmore Farm.

NORTH – Walk from Balquhidder on either (a) the narrow motor road W to Inverlochlarig running on the N shores of Lochs Voil and Doine, or (b) the forestry track on the S shores, crossing the river about 1½ miles W of Loch Doine to the motor road of (a). At Inverlochlarig, a scattered farm community, just at a picnic area the road forks. Take the R fork for ½ mile and enter the gate on the R opposite the first farmhouse. Go to the W end of the sheep pens to a gate which will bring you out on the open moor. The route is N up the Inverlochlarig Glen, a gentle climb up grassy slopes, almost lawn-like in their smoothness, by the side of the Inverlochlarig Burn.

Halfway up is a large 4m high boulder perching in midstream, a notable landmark. While the map shows tributaries, there is no mistaking the main course of the burn. Just before the saddle there is a handsome wide flat meadow through which the burn wanders. The saddle, at 500m, is humped in the middle and the way is on either side or over the hump (a cairn is on top of it). You are now looking down into Benmore Glen and you can choose your route down to the burn. At 12½ miles you reach a plantation on the W bank of the burn and here it is best to follow the forest fence almost to the A85. About ½ mile above the road the fence you have been following meets a cross-fence. Go over the first fence just N of the cross-fence and follow the latter W and then S down to the road about ¼ mile W of Benmore Farm. Crianlarich is 2 miles to the W on the A85.

SOUTH – Go E on the A85 out of Crianlarich to ¼ mile before Benmore Farm. Look for a ramp on the S side of the road, bordered by a wooden fence which leads up a few yards to gates. You want to be on the W side of a wire fence going uphill. This fence swings around E and crosses a forestry fence going N. You follow the E side of this second fence which will lead you to the upper reaches of the Benmore Glen along the W side of the burn. From the end of the forest you will be able to see a saddle due S. It is also possible to climb up the E side of the Benmore Burn, leaving the A85 at a point well beyond the farm buildings (a sign firmly discourages walkers from starting through the farmyard) and reaching the burn ¾ mile above the road. If there is mist, follow the burn until it peters out and the way steepens. Here go due S and the saddle will be gained in about ¼ mile. From the saddle the way down Glen Inverlochlarig is also due S, with the burn being picked up shortly after leaving the saddle. The narrow motor road to Balquhidder is reached at 9 miles and Balquhidder is 7 miles further along this road.

bracken

5 CRIANLARICH–BRIDGE OF ORCHY
12 miles (19km) 160ft (50m) OS 50

St Fillan's Chapel

This section is included for the purists who may wish to cover the route entirely on foot. The walk has magnificent views and several points of interest, though it passes along or near the tracks of the West Highland Railway and the A82, that busy road to Glencoe and the West. We recommend cheating by taking the train and enjoying the scenery guiltily but splendidly through its windows.

The use of public rather than private transport in your walking trip will colour the experience as much as your choice of which sections to walk. Any access to our Central Highlands Walk will entail some journeying on the West Highland line. This line, running from Glasgow to Mallaig, is probably the most spectacular train ride in Britain. A past journal of ours recounts our first experience of it.

Even before we clear the Glasgow suburbs the views are worth attention: the old Clyde–Forth Canal, now disused but still water-filled and with some of the old locks visible, then miles along the Clyde, up Gare Loch and over to Loch Long. The hills rise along the shores of Loch Long until they reach respectable heights. At Arrochar we swing over to Loch Lomond. Ben Lomond is partially hidden in clouds but the loch stretches away below us for miles. This is the way to see Loch Lomond. The crowded highway is below us, bringing back memories of past exasperations at being in one of those long queues behind caravans and lorries on that very road.

At Tyndrum we begin parting ways with the motor road, leaving it at the Bridge of Orchy to wend its way to Glencoe. Around us now spreads the desolation of Rannoch Moor, miles of peat bogs, tiny lochs, meandering streams and small hills. Deer graze by the dozens, one a silent sentinel against the skyline. A rainbow travels with us for 15 minutes on our right, growing to a complete arc and briefly becoming double before being extinguished. How welcoming! The far peaks grow ever more snow patched – we have come North!

But if you must walk this section, called Strathfillan, there are several points of interest associated with St Fillan, an eighth-century monk. By Kirkton Farmhouse are the ruins of a twelfth-century church with evidence of a sizable community: the remains of a rectangular enclosing garden wall, and a very old graveyard. It is thought that this chapel was a natural enlargement of the earlier site of St Fillan's original cell. A mile upstream is his Holy Pool used in healing ceremonies. At his death the saint was said to have entrusted five sacred relics to be watched over for ever; out of this grew the hereditary positions of the Dewars which persisted down into the seventeenth century. Two of the relics are purported to be a bell and a staff (Quiqrich) presently on display at Edinburgh Museum of Antiquities.

NORTH – Go N from Crianlarich on the A82 for about 2½ miles to the Kirkton Farm road, Go R and just before the farm buildings a path leads L along a fence past the ruins of St Fillan's Chapel and continues NW to Auchtertyre Farm. The Holy Pool is about 1 mile E up the Allt Gleann a'Chlachain from this farm. Go down the farm road to the A82 and continue N to Tyndrum (5½ miles), passing Dail Righ Farm on the L (site of a battle where Robert the Bruce narrowly escaped capture). Walk behind the village shop and take the old Glencoe road N. In about 1 mile it crosses the rly at the Crom Allt. You may return to the A82 and go N 2½ miles to the Auch Farm road or continue on the old road, having to cross the rly tracks where there is no bridge. From the Auch Farm the old road, in fair condition, goes N to the rly station at Bridge of Orchy. The hotel is on the A82 200yd downhill from the station.

SOUTH – Leave the A82 at the hotel and go E up to the rly station. Cross the tracks to the old road running S parallel to the tracks. From here follow the **NORTH** directions in reverse.

oak

6 BRIDGE OF ORCHY–KINGSHOUSE
11 miles (18km) 1098ft (335m) OS 41 & 50

Victoria Bridge

This section is mostly over the old military road built around 1750 or on the nineteenth-century carriage road which the modern A82 replaced in 1932. The way skirts Loch Tulla, crosses the wide moorland of the Black Mount, with views of the hills of the Black Mount to the west and the Grampian hills far to the east. It ends in the sombrely beautiful Glencoe. It is an easy walk in either direction, nicely leg-stretching if you have not 'walked-up' to condition, most of it being over open moor. We first walked it on a grey April day. The cloud cover to the east ended abruptly in a horizontal line, giving an odd cut-off effect as if a giant blind had been pulled down over the tops of the hills. We amused ourselves by speculating on the shapes and heights of those covered peaks. That and frequent stops for our son to 'finger-jog' the frogs which abounded in all the puddles were our only diversion from the pervasive message of the moor.

NORTH – From the station, follow the A8005 across the River Orchy towards Victoria Bridge and, at the bend in the road (¼ mile) immediately after you cross the bridge, a gate in a deer fence leads to a track slanting NW over Mam Carraigh to Inveroran Hotel on the A8005. From here follow the A8005 to Victoria Bridge and Forest Lodge (3 miles), where the carriage road (now private) carries on straight ahead through a gate. The old military road goes L off the carriage road just beyond the gate (here very faint but more visible

56

beyond the woods) and rejoins at 5¾ miles. You may take either route. From here the two roads are joined until beyond Ba Bridge where they again diverge. Ba Bridge and the ruins of Ba Cottage are the only man-made features on this length. Beyond Ba Cottage, the carriage and military roads climb the shoulder of a hill, and you will see Glencoe gradually unfold ahead. The military road goes sharp L at 8½ miles but is hard to find going N. Both roads come into the White Corries Chairlift road at 10 miles with Kingshouse Hotel a mile to the R across the A82.

SOUTH – Leave Kingshouse Hotel by its E access road, cross the A82 and go up the chairlift road. Just beyond the first house on the R (Black Rock Cottage), take the track to the L (carriage road). If the military road is to be followed, continue about ¼ mile further uphill. The latter joins the carriage road further on for several miles and is difficult to find when it diverges a second time. After joining the A8005 at Victoria Bridge, turn off in about a mile on a track uphill R (just after the Inveroran Hotel), over Mam Carraigh to Bridge of Orchy.

DIVERSION – For the hardy walkers there is a trackless diversion possible from Ba Bridge via a high pass between Aonach Mor and Clach Leathad. Leave the main section at Ba Bridge (7 miles from Bridge of Orchy, 320m) and go up the River Ba to its headwaters, over a high saddle at 670m dropping down A Coire Ghuibhasan to the River Etive and the Glen Etive road (14½ miles, 120m). Go R on this road to the A82 (19 miles) and Kingshouse (20 miles). A long day for strong scramblers and not recommended in mist or high winds.

7 KINGSHOUSE–KINLOCHLEVEN
9 miles (14½km) 1780ft (540m) OS 41

This is a short section mostly over the old military road. It climbs 270m out of Glencoe by the famous 'Devil's Staircase', a series of sharp switchbacks difficult for even an adder to negotiate. One can imagine the feeling of Redcoat cannoneers or waggoners getting their charges up or down, on their way to quell a Highland 'disturbance'. From the top of the 'Staircase', at 540m altitude, the road crosses a small valley containing the ruins of a summer shieling and drops steadily and sometimes steeply to sea level at Loch Leven. There are excellent views into Glencoe from the 'Staircase', and as the road descends north from the ridge, the Blackwater Reservoir stretches out to the east. The way is easier northbound because Kinlochleven is 244m lower than Kingshouse.

Our first experience of this section was as the second day of a 12-day walk. Having plodded into Kingshouse from Rannoch Station the day before, our legs still weak from the sudden return to hiking, we welcomed both the shortness of the walk and the fact that after the initial climb it was easy going. While toiling up the switchbacks in the rain, our senses were suddenly jarred out of the romantic vision of those men of the past struggling with their wheeled equipment by the recent imprint of modern wheels. Motorcycle tracks! How affronted we felt at this evidence of noisy engines traversing what we thought the peaceful province of walkers only. Abruptly, greater insight was given us into the sense of outrage those Highlanders of the past must have felt against the builders and users of the famous military roads in

18th century intruder

20th century intruder

the area. The single person we saw during the walk explained to us the reason for the tracks – an annual motorcycle race, held since 1911. Lucky we were to miss it! If you plan to go during the first two weeks of May, check on the day and time of this race with the local tourist board.

NORTH – Go W up the glen from Kingshouse Hotel on its W access road to the A82 and on to Altnafeadh (2½ miles). The military road runs parallel with the motor road for much of this distance but is difficult to follow. At Altnafeadh a track goes R just to the L of a white house, through a small stand of pines. You climb steeply NW by the 'Devil's Staircase' to a ridge at 3½ miles. From the ridge the track descends steadily with good footing, passing a waterfall on the L at 5 miles and a small loch on the R at 7 miles. A number of rivulets crossing the track are welcome thirst slakers, some reached without even bending. The track reaches the A82 just by Kinlochleven.

SOUTH – Leave the town car park on the S side of the River Leven and head uphill around a large deserted white house. Then contour E until a path is picked up running to join the track coming down SE to the aluminium works. Once on this track the way is clear to the A82 at Altnafeadh, from where the Kingshouse Hotel is 2½ miles to the L.

8 KINLOCHLEVEN–FORT WILLIAM
15 miles (24km) 920ft (290m) OS 41

'Failte!'

This is a long but easy walk, two-thirds of it over the old military road and the remainder over an unfrequented motor road. It climbs briefly out of Kinlochleven and winds through the deserted narrow valley of the Allt na Lairige Moire, lined by high hills, around the bulk of Meall a'Chaorainn, and along the wider Strath Kiachnish down to Fort William. The massive dome of Ben Nevis is much in view during the **NORTH** walk. The military road is in good repair and you should note the cobble construction where burns are guided across the road – withstanding freshets for 200 years.

As we climbed out of Kinlochleven one crisp sunny morning, we looked back and remembered earlier impressions received when driving through – of a cheerless and uniform 'company' town dominated by a massive aluminium works. How different it was to walk in, meet and stay with warm-hearted people, view the many pleasant gardens and houses away from the through traffic and to see the town life through the eyes of the locals. We had known so little of the town beforehand that we had written blind to the Postmaster for advice about accommodation. In return we received a cordial reply from a pensioner family with our own surname! On acquaintance, our landlady proved to be a kindly transplanted Londoner, her husband a local man who 'had the Gaelic' as a first language and who possessed a fund of stories. So Kinlochleven came alive for us and we looked back with pleasure as we left.

NORTH – Go N from Kinlochleven by the A82 around the head of the loch. In ¾ mile you will find the footpath to Fort William signposted. The path struggles up the slope for about a mile to meet an LRT coming from the R. Go L and the LRT turns into the old military road. At 4½ miles Tigh na sluebhaich, still occasionally lived in, is passed and at 5½ miles the ruins of Lairigmor are left behind. The way continues uneventfully down a now-deserted valley to a plantation at 7½ miles and a motor road at 9 miles. Fort William is 6 miles straight ahead.

For those using the Glen Nevis Youth Hostel, a track leads E (R) about a mile from Fort William. It goes over the N shoulder of Beinn Riabhach to the Glen Nevis motor road, where the hostel is a mile to the R. This detour adds about 2 miles to the journey.

SOUTH – Leave Fort William rly station and walk S through the town to the roundabout (½ mile). Here a road goes L uphill through a housing development and in another mile leaves civilisation mostly behind. At 6 miles the motor road bends sharp R and an unmarked forest road continues straight ahead, becoming the military road to Kinlochleven. About a mile before Kinlochleven watch for a narrow path going off R downhill to the A82 just W of Kinlochleven. If this is missed, the way you are on becomes an LRT to Mamore Lodge, where you can take the estate road down to the A82 and then turn L to Kinlochleven.

spring
uncurling

ALTERNATIVE SECTIONS (track data given in one direction only). There are numerous one-day walks off this route. We have chosen three, one because of its challenge, one because of its sheer scenic beauty and one which includes the option of a climb up a 'Munro', a peak over 910m.

1a KINLOCHARD–ROWARDENNAN (via Ben Lomond)
12 miles (19km) 3190ft (970m) OS 56 & 57

This is a pleasant walk over a shoulder of Ben Lomond to the shores of Loch Lomond, with the option of including a climb to the top of Ben Lomond. It is a somewhat more interesting start or finish to the Central Highland Route than the Drymen–Kinlochard section, but it can be done in the summer season only, when there is a train and steamer to Rowardennan from Glasgow. The steamer ride on Loch Lomond is an attraction in itself. The footing is fair to good, the way well marked.

WEST – Go around the N end of Kinlochard. Just beyond the housing area, a signpost points the way to 'Rowardennan via Ben Lomond 1200ft, 8½ miles'. The walk is marked by *red* chevrons on posts (note: posts will be found *beyond* any forks in the path, requiring a bit of trial and error in pathfinding). The way moves above the loch, entering the Loch Ard Forest, and follows first the Duchray Water and then a tributary, coming out into the open at about 6 miles. At 7 miles the path to the top of Ben Lomond is reached, with the summit 1¾ miles to the N (miss it if you are tired or the weather is bad). If you climb it, and the views are tremendous in clear weather, you will return to this spot from which the path goes 1½ miles downhill to Rowardennan.

7a RANNOCH STATION–KINGSHOUSE
12 miles (19km) 380ft (115m) OS 41 & 51

This is a walk across Rannoch Moor, a desolate and forbidding land of lochs and bogs. It is largely trackless and tiring to walk because of the boggy footing, but it is rewarding in its vast sweep of moor and sky and its challenge in bog-trotting.

WEST – Leave Rannoch rly station and go along the NW shore of Loch Laidon (avoid the LRT into the forest above). At the ruins of Tighe na Cruaiche (4 miles) turn due W from the loch. The Black Corries bulk on your R. A line of power pylons march parallel to your way but at some distance up the slope of the Black Corries (in mist these can be followed). At about 7 miles and with thoroughly wet feet you will encounter an old track leading to the Black Corries Lodge at 9 miles. Here the estate road leads down to Kingshouse Hotel.

highland cattle

8a FORT WILLIAM–CORROUR
20 miles (32km) (12½ miles + taxi) 1300ft (400m) OS 41

This is a very long walk. It passes between Fort William and the remote rly station at Corrour through the magnificent Glen Nevis under the great massif of Ben Nevis, Britain's highest mountain. The walk extends the route another worthwhile day. You have the option of starting or ending the walk at Corrour because there is a morning and evening train from both directions (none on Sunday). There is only a Youth Hostel at Corrour.

EAST – Go N on the A82 from the rly station in Fort William a short distance to the motor road to Glen Nevis. At 7½ miles the road ends and a path continues along the N bank of the Water of Nevis. In about 4 miles (11½ miles from Fort William) the highest point of land is passed at Tom an Eite and the path goes down the S bank of the Abhain Rath to the head of Loch Treig at 16 miles. Follow the S shore of the loch for about 1½ miles. Just beyond the bridge over the Allt a Chamabhreac take a track leading R to Corrour Station in 2½ miles.

ARGYLL WALK Grampians
30/36 miles (48/58km)

SECTION	DISTANCE		OVERNIGHT POINTS
1	9m	(14½km)	Strachur-Lochgoilhead
2	9-15m	(14½-24km)	Lochgoilhead-Arrochar
3	12m	(19km)	Arrochar-Ardlui

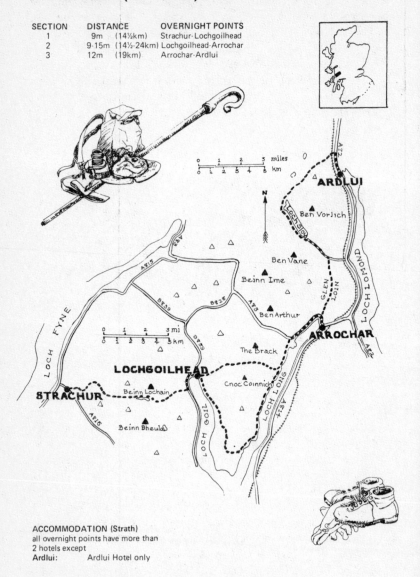

ACCOMMODATION (Strath)
all overnight points have more than
2 hotels except
Ardlui: Ardlui Hotel only

PUBLIC TRANSPORT (H&I)
Strachur: bus Dunoon (Mon-Sat); ferry & train Dunoon-Glasgow
Lochgoilhead: bus Tarbet; train Tarbet-Glasgow (Mon-Sat)
Arrochar: bus Glasgow or bus Tarbet; train Tarbet to Glasgow (Mon-Sat)
Ardlui: bus or train Glasgow, Fort William or Oban

64

This Walk goes through Argyll, the early Scots kingdom of Dalriada. It was in this country, now so peaceful, that the invading Scots from Ireland secured a foothold against the little-known but powerful Picts. The Scots, the Normans of their day, by force of arms and guile imposed their control and finally their name on Scotland.

The sea bites deeply here, with sea lochs running many miles inland. The Walk makes a great crescent, from the shores of Loch Fyne to fabled Loch Lomond, through a series of hills and mountain ranges and by the shores of fjord-like Loch Goil and Loch Long. The way passes through the Arrochar Alps, many of the peaks reaching over 900m. There is more variety in footing than on other routes. The way travels the usual roads, forest rides, hill tracks and footpaths but also edges along a steep-sided fresh-water loch wedged between two high peaks and runs along on top of an old covered aqueduct. After many visits we still find ourselves surprised that this kind of spectacular scenery and quiet remoteness has survived its close proximity to busy industrialised Glasgow. It is a popular area, but all the visitors, except for walkers or the inhabitants themselves, touch only the edges of its beauty, spectators rather than participants.

The walks are easy to moderately strenuous, the footing poor to excellent and the way well marked to pathless, but they can be done by walkers with little experience. Two of the overnight points, Arrochar and Ardlui, are reached by direct train from Glasgow in about 1½ hours.

OVERNIGHT POINTS – Strachur is a small village near the shore of Loch Fyne on the Cowal peninsula and was the seat of the McArthur Campbells. The old part of the village, with its handsome church, is ½ mile from the loch. The hotels are along the shore. **Lochgoilhead** is a village at the head of Loch Goil, a short, narrow loch diverging from Loch Long. There is a static caravan park and a cluster of new chalets a mile away but they do not spoil the quiet village aspect. The local area is wooded and there are several short walks out of the village among flowering shrubs and large trees. **Arrochar** is a village at the head of Loch Long, with some of the finest peaks, the Arrochar Alps, to the northwest. The best known is Ben Arthur or 'The Cobbler'. The views of these and of Loch Long make it a favourite 'stop and look' spot for motorists, thus an easier place to find food and lodging than most villages here. **Ardlui** is situated at the head of Loch Lomond and the entrance to Glen Falloch and has a few houses, a hotel and a railway station. It lies along the busy road of Lomondside but a few steps towards the loch or the hills and you will forget the traffic.

1 STRACHUR–LOCHGOILHEAD
9 miles (14½km) 985ft (300m) OS 56

forgetmenot

birdsfoot trefoil

orchid

tormentil

This is a short but moderately strenuous walk over the hills of the Glenbranter Forest in Argyll Forest Park. The way is between two sea lochs, from the village of Strachur on the shore of Loch Fyne to the head of Loch Goil. It is a grand beginning or end to the 3-day route. Strachur is somewhat difficult to reach by public transport, requiring a train, ferry and bus from Glasgow but the scenery en route is worth the trouble. The way is well marked, the footing good to poor, with a few boggy places.

EAST – Leave Strachur by the A815 towards Dunoon. In about ¾ mile turn L at a signpost to 'Succoth'; In ½ mile turn L again (straight ahead goes to Strachurmore Farm). There follows rather more than a mile of narrow country road through a pleasant glen lined with deciduous woods. Within sight of Succothmore Farm leave the road by a forest track striking off R over a wooden bridge. The track goes through a gate and shortly joins a hard-surfaced forest road. Bear L on this and walk uphill for about a mile (a burn is below you on your L). Take a L fork slanting down towards the burn. This bit of track is an old disused road and it peters out by the burn. It is important not to miss this fork since the surfaced road will merely take you on a wide circuit of Beinn Lagan to hit the A815 some 4 miles from Strachur – a pleasant walk but not the object of this exercise. Across the burn (some agility needed here if you want to avoid wet feet) can be seen the first of a line of guide posts which you will follow until you reach the shores of Loch Goil. At this point they stretch E over the lower slopes of Cruach na Cioba. There is not much of a path but the signposts are easy to see. The burn is now on the R and the markers follow its course to the Bealach an Lochain. This is a watershed and the going gets wetter. Just over the bealach is Curra Lochain, a stretch of water about a half-mile long. The path skirts the L bank over very wet ground and at the end of the loch it is forced down to the water's edge by a boundary fence. It then starts the descent through plantations of spruce and larch to the Lettermay Burn. Before descending, look NE to the rocky summit of Ben Arthur (The Cobbler) 7½ miles distant, and S where the Lettermay Burn rises in the cirque formed by the crags of Beinn Bheula. The distance to be covered in descending to the burn is only about a mile but unless the walker is equipped with a short left leg and webbed feet, progress is likely to be very slow. The track makes a long traverse across a steeply sloping hillside where the surface is as wet and muddy as can be and there are dirty scrambles over awkward outcrops of rocks. The Lettermay Burn is crossed by a substantial wooden bridge and a few minutes later one thankfully gains the firm footing of a forest road. This leads down past Lettermay Farm to the public road which skirts the W shore of Loch Goil. Go L 1½ miles to Lochgoilhead.

WEST – From Lochgoilhead walk around the head of the loch, passing on the way a large caravan park beyond which a profusion of modern chalets covers the hillside. In 1½ miles turn R to the Lettermay Farm where on the L is a Forestry Commission notice board marking the start of a forest road and indicating the colour code used to mark the walks that can be followed. In less than a mile a sign points R and there are posts to guide you down to the Lettermay Burn and then by a muddy track up the wooded hillside to Curra Lochain. The track skirts the N shore and then descends gently from the watershed. There is a burn on your L which swings N across your front. Ford it (by this time your feet are soaking wet anyway) and bear R up the opposite bank until you hit a forest road. Go R on this for about a mile, then cross the River Cur by a wooden bridge and continue L down the valley to the A815. Strachur is ¾ mile to the R.

celandine

anemone

wood·sorrel

2 LOCHGOILHEAD–ARROCHAR
9–15 miles (14½–24km) 1600ft (490m) OS 56

Loch Goil

Here is a walker's choice of a short or long walk over the Ardgartan Forest, a long finger of high ground between Loch Long and Loch Goil. It is handsome country, with steep hills cut by long narrow sea lochs. There are extensive forest plantations and the way is partly along forest roads. The steepness of the land allows almost constant views even in the forests. The way is easy and marked by painted posts, the footing good to excellent. We left Glasgow early one rainy morning to do this section. The bus was full of youngsters on their way to an outdoor centre and their irrepressible spirits and cheerful songs lightened what to walkers was a gloomy day. By Loch Lomond they had stopped the rain and by Arrochar had got the sun to shine on the Cobbler. Here we left them to continue their highly effective anti-rain songs and spent the day walking under clear skies.

WEST – Leave Arrochar on the A83, going N around the head of Loch Long (good views of the Cobbler) and then S to Ardgartan at 2½ miles. Here the motor road turns away from the loch. At 3 miles take a tarmac road L across the river Croe. Go R 100yd to a point marked 'Forest Walk' on the map and then L (S) on a tarmac road along Loch Long for 2 miles to Coilessan. At this point there are two choices: (a) up Coilessan Glen and down to Lochgoilhead, or (b) a longer and more strenuous walk which almost circumnavigates the long finger of land between the two lochs. For (a) turn W on an unpaved forest road going up the glen, marked by blue-painted posts. The road climbs steadily for about 1 mile through forest and then goes steeply up an open slope for another mile to the saddle between the Brack and Cnoc Coinnich (7 miles, 490m). Here there are good views back to Loch Long and ahead to Loch Goil. Mist need not deter you from crossing the saddle as long as an approximate W compass heading is kept. The slopes on either side of the saddle are grassy for some distance from the line of your walk, safely negotiable if you should stray off the path. The path descends from the saddle less steeply than the ascent, to a forest edge where it joins a path coming in from the R from Glen Croe (white-painted posts). The way is now through pine and larch to Lochgoilhead. A burn is crossed by a wooden bridge (worth a rest here). The way now alternates between forest roads and paths but is easy to follow because of the painted guide-posts. Lochgoilhead is reached at 9 miles.

For the longer choice (b), continue S along Loch Long on an unpaved forest road with yellow-painted posts. The road climbs up to Corran Lochan. Beyond, an ill-defined and rather boggy path goes up through a pass at 305m between the Saddle and Tom Molach, descending to a forest road that takes you comfortably into Lochgoilhead, 15 miles from Arrochar.

EAST – The walks above can readily be followed in the reverse direction from Lochgoilhead to Arrochar. Start from the car park in the village and walk about 100yd N to a gate where a Forestry Commission notice-board marks the start of the walks, giving the colours that you must look for on the guideposts.

wild foxglove

3 ARROCHAR–ARDLUI
12 miles (19km) 1200ft (365m) OS 56

Ardlui

This is a moderately strenuous walk through the Arrochar Alps by the passes of Glen Loin and Glen Sloy, from Loch Long to Loch Lomond. The way is lined by mountains, with fine views of three Munros, Ben Vorlich (943m), Ben Vane (916m), Beinn Narnain (926m) and a glimpse of Beinn Ime (1011m). This walk is never dull as there is a variety of landscapes and footing as well as a small challenge in path-finding near Ardlui. Except for the latter, the way is easily followed. The footing is poor to excellent.

NORTH – Go N from Arrochar on the A83 for ½ mile. Just before the stone bridge at the head of the loch, take an unpaved road that goes R along the E side of Loin Water. At Stronafyne (a farm and caravans) go R through the farmyard and continue N on an LRT. When this comes to an end, follow the faint track going in the same direction up Glen Loin. Keep the power pylons on your L as you climb until you are nearly abreast of the small hump of Dubh Chnoc. From here you will get a fine view of Ben Vorlich and Ben Vane. Beyond this point choose your own way down to the road to Sloy Dam. The most direct way is down under the line of pylons and, moving parallel to them, cross the Inverglas Water which flows here through a small wooded glen. If the Water is in spate, you will have to swing NW ¼ mile and cross the bridge shown on the map. Go NW up the dam access road to Loch Sloy (reached by a short tunnel at the top, or, if nervous about rocks falling off the tunnel roof onto your head, by walking across the top of the tunnel). Ahead of you, Loch Sloy stretches for 2 miles.

There is no path but either side is negotiable. If the water level is high you will walk along the steep grassy slopes of Beinn Dhubh on the W shore or of Ben Vorlich on the E shore. If the water level is low, there are sandy terraces below the grass for much of the way, with occasional scrambles across small ravines made by burns. A drowned ruin of a cottage may be visible above the water near the head of the loch. We were there in a drought and the ruin was entirely above water and could be visited, melancholy in its coat of grime. At the head of the loch you can either head NW to an LRT ¼ mile above the loch and go NE on the LRT to a point ¼ mile before it crosses the Srath Dubh-uisge, or walk by rather boggy ground along the burn flowing into the head of the loch to the same point (9 miles from Arrochar). Here you will find what at first glance looks like an abandoned rly going NE parallel to the burn but well above it. It will soon become evident that it is a large turf-covered concrete aqueduct. Walk along its top for about 1 mile until it disappears abruptly into the hillside. From this point pick your way down the N bank of Srath Dubh-uisge. As the way steepens, move away from the streambed and keep to steep but negotiable bracken-covered slopes down to the rly. There is a small bridge over the rly, as shown on the OS map. Cross this bridge to the A82 a short distance beyond. Ardlui is 1 mile to the R.

SOUTH – Walk N from Ardlui 1 mile to the first substantial bridge. 200yd beyond, there is a field on your L with a sign 'Arab Forestry Estate'. Leave the A82 here, cross a small bridge over the rly and toil W up the steep slope on the N side of Srath Dubh-uisge. As the slope flattens, choose a dry contour above the burn and go SW to an LRT which crosses the valley. Take the LRT SW until opposite the head of Loch Sloy then go along either side of the loch to the dam. Go down the dam access road to the second track on R (Coiregrogain) and cross a bridge over Inverglas Water to a faint track L round the foot of Dubh Chnoc and by an intermittent track over to and down Glen Loin to the A83 and Arrochar.

larch

BREADALBANE WALK Grampians
38 miles (61km)

SECTION	DISTANCE		OVERNIGHT POINTS
1	10m	(16km)	Strathyre-Lochearnhead
2	15m	(24km)	Lochearnhead-Callander
3	13m	(21km)	Callander-Comrie

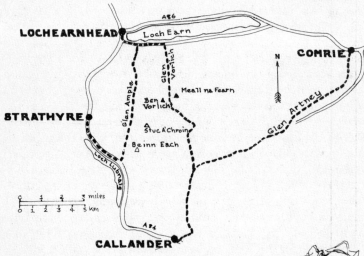

PUBLIC TRANSPORT (H&I except Comrie which is WAS)
Strathyre
Lochearnhead } bus Stirling; train Stirling to Glasgow & Edinburgh
Callander
Comrie: bus Crieff; bus Crieff to Stirling

ACCOMMODATION (Cent except Comrie
which is Tay)
(except as noted below, overnight points
have more than 2 hotels)
Comrie: Comrie Hotel, Royal Hotel,
                Mossgiel Guest House

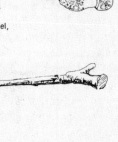

We were drawn to this Walk by Scott's marvellous lines at the beginning of his 'Lady of the Lake':

> The stag at eve had drunk his fill
> where danced the moon on Monan's rill
> and deep his midnight lair had made
> In lone Glenartney's hazel shade;
>
> But when the sun his beacon red
> Had kindled on Benvorlich's head,
> The deep-mouthed bloodhounds' heavy bay
> Resounded up the rocky way
> And faint, from farther distance born
> Were heard the clanging hoof and horn

and we thought of that wonderful imagery as we walked along. The way passes on both sides of Ben Vorlich (not to be confused with the one in the Arrochar Alps to the west) so you see the mountain from every aspect. The Walk ends in 'Glenartney's hazel shade' by walking through its quiet woods. The area is bounded by Loch Earn on the north, Loch Lubnaig on the west and the Teith valley on the south and, within these bounds, it is mostly uninhabited moorland laced by tumbling burns. This is the country through which Scott's hunters first pursued the stag, dropping out one by one until, far beyond at the edge of Loch Katrine, the boldest lost the stag and his horse but found his 'lady of the lake.'

OVERNIGHT POINTS – Strathyre is a village named after the strath running N–S between two high ridges. A variety of buildings, mostly old, lines each side of the road and provides more than adequate amenities. Just south is Loch Lubnaig, an unspoiled, narrow, dog-legged loch popular with picnickers and fishermen. **Lochearnhead** is a popular resort village on the west end of Loch Earn. The view of the loch from here is especially fine. Nearby is ruined St Blane's Chapel. **Callander** is one of the busiest tourist towns in Scotland, its main street lined with shops and people. It is known as the Gateway to the Highlands. There are pleasant short walks if you stay over a day, the Crags and Bracklinn Falls being the best known. There is a 1753 sundial in South Church Street. **Comrie** is a small town in Strathearn popular with summer visitors rather than passing motorists. Its main street has attractive old buildings housing interesting shops. Comrie Church, built in 1805, has a steeple designed by John Stewart.

1 STRATHYRE–LOCHEARNHEAD
10 miles (16km) 770ft (235m) OS 51 & 57

Ardchullarie

Most of this walk is across upland pastures lying between Loch Lubnaig and Loch Earn. Ben Vorlich rises above you and the summit can be reached from your route. The views are superb and add to the feeling of peace and openness which prevail throughout the walk. The two lochs are different in character and in their surrounding countryside but alike in presenting a beautiful aspect to the walker whether seen as you come down to their shores or looking back as you climb away from them. Loch Lubnaig is the smaller of the two and the hills rise more steeply from it. No houses or hotels are along its shores and, except for the A84 running alongside with a number of fine picnic areas, there is no evidence of human intrusion. Loch Earn, on the other hand, has a large hotel at one end and shops and services. Both its shores gives access to the water and, although not teeming with activity, there are generally white sails dotting its blue surface and evidence of other human use. Not too much incursion on man's part but just enough to welcome you back from the solitude of the hills.

This is an easy walk, the footing good to excellent and the way clearly marked. Because of the section of road walking at each end, care should be exercised as to when you do this walk. The 2½ miles from Strathyre are on a busy road from Callander, a popular weekend run from Glasgow and Edinburgh. We walked it on a Sunday during Whitsun so it is not surprising that we found it busy. The mile along the southern shore of Loch Earn is less busy, although we were amazed

74

at how many cars were using this narrow road which has so little room for passing. You will often find yourself leaping off into the bushes; not a pleasant experience, especially when you have come off the hills where you share the way only with the sheep and the birds. We did go back another time and found it deserted, so obviously the answer is to choose your day of the week wisely or, if you must do it at a weekend, to make an early start.

NORTH – Leave Strathyre and walk S on the A84 for 2½ miles to Ardchullarie More Farm where the way is signposted to Edinample. The A84 is a winding, busy road with little verge, so walk defensively. If starting by bus from either the N or S, Ardchullarie More Farm is halfway along Loch Lubnaig (in case the bus driver is not familiar with the area).

The whole way from Ardchullarie More to Edinample is well worn and you should have no difficulty in finding the path. It follows a N–S direction along the Ample Burn for most of its way. There is a steep ascent from Loch Lubnaig and it is a pleasure to reach the top of the climb and traverse the wide high pasture land until it comes to Glenample Farm. At only one point, where the way turns through a gate uphill away from the burn, is the path momentarily erased by grassy turf but there is a yellow-painted marker stake to show where it continues up the hillside. At Glenample you have the choice of crossing immediately to the W side of the burn by the new footbridge or continuing on the E side to the bridge and ford further down. From here the track takes you down to Edinample and the road running along the S shore of Loch Earn. Go L on this road to the A84. Lochearnhead is to the R, 1½ miles from Edinample.

SOUTH – Walk S from Lochearnhead on the A84 to the South Loch Earn Road (so marked). Go E on this road and you will come to Edinample (1½ miles) with a castle on your L and the way marked to Loch Lubnaig on your R. Take this track up the hill past Glenample Farm and on through the glen, coming down to the A84 again at Ardchullarie More. Strathyre is 2½ miles to the R.

please close!

75

2 LOCHEARNHEAD–CALLANDER
15 miles (24km) 1970ft (600m) OS 51 & 57

curlew

This is mostly a moorland walk by two high passes on the east flank of Ben Vorlich, with views of Loch Earn to the north and the broad valley of the Teith to the south. There is a long pathless stretch that is easy to follow in clear weather with a longer alternative in case of mist. There is almost no reafforestation so that you have a feeling of walking through land unchanged for a thousand years. The footing is fair to excellent, the way not too difficult to find.

We did this walk during the height of the nesting season and parent birds were busy trying to distract us or drive us away. A meadow pipit ran across our path doing a piteous broken-wing act that would have wrung tears from a stone. A duo of curlews dive-bombed us until our scalps prickled in anticipation of their long bills raking our heads. A mother red grouse scurried away from us, enticing us to chase her, while her dozen chicks scattered in the opposite direction. We watched the chicks disappear into the heather and spent a cautious 15 minutes lifting heather branches before we found even one chick, so well camouflaged were they. Careful not to touch it, we clicked our camera busily while it pretended we were not there. It was also here that we saw our first black grouse, a much rarer bird than the common red grouse. It is considerably larger than the red and when one exploded into flight from under our feet, a rocket of black and white feathers, we were nearly scared to death. We later did a bit of reading on the special social behaviour of this species and we would like to be present some early spring morning at a 'lek', their dance ground, to watch the blackcocks go through their formalised ritual dance in concert.

SOUTH – Walk S from Lochearnhead on the A84 for ½ mile to the South Loch Earn Road (signposted). Go E for 3 miles to the E gate of Ardvorlich Estate (signposted to Ben Vorlich) and take the track along the W side of the Glen Vorlich burn. In about ¾ mile, a faint track goes L from the well-used main track as the latter swings away from the burn. Take this L fork and continue S up the burn. The track disappears but you will follow the burn up to a notch between Ben Vorlich and Meall na Fearn (the notch is close to Ben Vorlich's flank). Go S from the notch down to Dubh Choirein where two burns join to form the Allt an Dubh Choirein. Here take a branch of the Allt SW uphill to a saddle between Meall na h-Iolaire and the long southern ridge of Stuc a Chroin. Go S from this saddle across the W slope of Meall Odhar (here you can pick up a good sheep track about 200yd above and parallel to a fence) down to Ardvurichardich (10¼ miles). Beyond the deserted farmhouse you will hit an LRT going S down to Braeleny (12½ miles) and a narrow paved road to Callander. In the event that mist covers the saddle between Meall na h-Iolaire and Stuc a Chroin, we recommend that you go SE down the Allt an Dubh Choirein to an LRT going W to Ardvurichardich. This adds about 2 miles to the walk.

NORTH – From Callander walk E on the A84 from its junction with the A81 to Bracklinn Avenue (signposted 'To Golf Course and Bracklinn Falls') and go L. Follow signs to Bracklinn Falls, which will put you firmly on the road to Braeleny. Continue beyond Braeleny to Ardvurichardich and go through a gate on to pastureland. Head N up the W slope of Meall Odhar to the most prominent N–S sheep track above and parallel to the highest fence. In a mile or so the track peters out but the saddle to the W of Meall na h-Iolaire will be visible ahead. Go over the saddle and down along a burn to Dubh Choirein and up the burn that passes to the E of Ben Vorlich (do not go up the enclosed valley of the main branch of the burn, marked as Gleann an Dubh Choirein, a possible but unlikely mistake). At the head of the burn you will see a V-shaped notch ahead, leading down Glen Vorlich to the road along the S shore of Loch Earn. Lochearnhead is to the L. The way is trackless from the saddle by Meall na h-Iolaire to near Loch Earn, but the burns furnish ample guidance.

blackcock
at lek

3 CALLANDER–COMRIE
13 miles (21km) 935ft (285m) OS 51 & 57

This is a long but easy walk from the busy holiday centre of Callander to the quiet small town of Comrie, by way of moorlands and the wooded Glen Artney. It affords contrasts in overnight points and in the terrain covered. The way is by unfrequented roads, LRTs and farm tracks. As you walk through quiet high pastures, it is hard to remember that the busy town of Callander lies close at hand but out of sight under the hill. Again one has the feeling of being favoured over those who are tied to their cars and coaches and who never walk by the hour in these surroundings. The way between Callander and Glen Artney is largely through a grouse moor. As we walked through it we realised how little we knew about grouse; later we did a bit of reading. In the investigations on moorland ecology carried on by Aberdeen University there has been considerable research done on grouse. It has been shown that the numbers and breeding success of the grouse depend on the quantity and quality of the heather available. This in turn depends on (besides weather conditions) how the landowner manages his land in regard to burning and grazing. Started as a study of grouse, the investigators had to enlarge their view to include the natural history of the whole moorland. Darlington and Boyd in their book *The Highlands and Islands* have a beautiful phrase for this inter-relationship: 'the living web of the moorland'.

Grouse cocks take up territories in the autumn and hold them through to the spring. The younger, more aggressive, birds have the best and largest territories, ousting the older and less fit ones. Territories are fiercely defended and surplus birds expelled. The hens wander around in small flocks while this jockeying for position goes on but, as winter progresses, they move into the territories and in late winter breeding pairs are established. You may feel that all grouse are alike but the cocks at least come in three classes; married property owners, the same unmarried, and those disadvantaged drifters who wander over poor land or trespass on others' territory. There is a constant change of position each autumn, however, and since only healthy birds are able to hold territory, there is a process of natural selection taking place. Now the next time you flush up a seemingly indistinguishable cock bird you may contemplate which member of the hierarchy you are disturbing. Continuing the walk, the way through Glen Artney is by farm tracks high above the Water of Ruchill, past ploughed fields, through deciduous forests and by deserted farm buildings. The way is easy to find, the footing good to excellent.

NORTHEAST – From Callander walk E on the A84 from its junction with the A81 to Bracklinn Avenue (signposted 'To Golf Course and Bracklinn Falls') and go L. Follow signs to Bracklinn Falls, which will put you firmly on the road up to Braeleny. From Braeleny an LRT goes N to a ford and bridge over Keltie Water (4 miles). Shortly after crossing the Water another LRT goes R, signposted as a public footpath to Comrie. If you walk this in spring and early summer the lapwings and curlews will entertain you as they fly up all around you, their distinctive calls breaking the prevailing silence. There is little change in elevation but the surrounding countryside changes from rolling grassy hills to more deeply indented heather-clad ones. The change of vegetation brings with it a profusion of grouse blinds and a whirring into the air of many of the future sacrificial victims. The LRT descends to cross a bridge over an impressive steep and narrow gorge through which flows Allt an Dubh Choirein. There is a return of rolling pastures at this point and in a short while the LRT ends at the Glen Artney Estate road with a sign marking the route by which you have just come. Go through a white gate to the road. On the other side of the road is a building marked 'Staghorne'. Go L past this building along the road to a track going R past Auchinner. Continue on to a bridge over the Allt Srath a Ghlinne just before it reaches the Water of Ruchill. Cross and go E on a track high above the river. It peters out in ½ mile and you continue parallel to the river on a sheep track along a stone wall. In another ½ mile you reach an LRT which you follow until it swings N at Dalclathick. Here an unused track continues parallel to the river, passing the ruins of a house in a few yards. This track, winding through deep woods and open fields, is charming in mist or sun. It carries through to the farm at Dalrannoch (13 miles) where a narrow paved road goes down to the A85 in Comrie. The town centre is to the R.

SOUTHWEST – Leave Comrie town centre and go W on the A85 till you come to a signpost to Dalrannoch. Go L and follow the **NORTHEAST** directions in reverse.

red grouse

PERTHSHIRE WALK Grampians
34 miles (54km)

SECTION	DISTANCE		OVERNIGHT POINTS
1	9m	(14km)	Blair Atholl-Pitlochry
2	10m	(16km)	Pitlochry-Kirkmichael
3	15m	(24km)	Kirkmichael-Dunkeld

PUBLIC TRANSPORT (H&I)
Blair Atholl
Pitlochry } train or bus Edinburgh, Glasgow or Inverness
Dunkeld
Kirkmichael: none

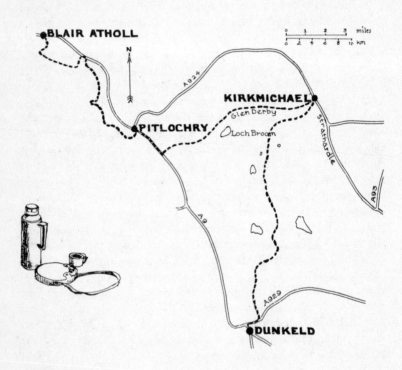

ACCOMMODATION (Tay)
(except as noted below, overnight points have more than 2 hotels)
Kirkmichael: Kirkmichael Hotel, The Log Cabin Hotel, Ardlebrig B&B

80

This part of Scotland offers high open vistas of moorland, with small villages and good-sized towns lying in the more fertile valley below. The Walk will generally be in splendid solitude. Your overnight stops will be more varied: the lively town of Pitlochry, the tiny hamlet of Kirkmichael, the restored village of Dunkeld, or isolated farm B&Bs. The walks themselves are through rolling upland pastures and moors, with views of mountains stretching along the horizon to the north. The slopes of the moors are often thick with heather, a bleak blackish sight in early spring turning to a soft pink and lavender one in the summer months.

Despite the evidence of man's presence in pastures and LRTs, you see few of your fellow humans beyond the farmhouses, generally walking all day with only cattle and sheep for company. In spring there will be mostly shy ewes with one or two lambs busily nursing, their little tails rotating like propellers. It is a paradise for birds – the curlew, lapwings, and meadow pipits especially.

OVERNIGHT POINTS – Pitlochry is one of the best-known Highland resort towns, in a wooded setting on the River Tummel. It claims to be the exact centre of Scotland. The Pitlochry Festival Theatre presents plays during the summer months, while there is fishing and a wealth of short walks in the neighbourhood. There is an excellent display of a salmon ladder here; don't miss it. It is encouraging to see an example of man's ability, as he pursues modernization, to cooperate with nature rather than destroy it. **Blair Atholl** is a village standing on the River Garry, among woods, hills and moors. Blair Castle (open to the public) is an old seat of the Clan Murray and dates back to 1269. It stands in an extensive park, the interior being noted for its period furniture, weapons and other relics. **Dunkeld** is an ancient little cathedral town beautifully situated in the well-wooded valley of the Tay, where it is crossed by a seven-arched bridge erected by Telford in 1809. The town was heavily damaged in 1689 in a siege by Highlanders fighting for the restoration of James II against King William. Some 40 houses, dating from the rebuilding after this siege, were restored in 1950–55 by the National Trust for Scotland. The Cathedral, partially restored, still dominates the town. The restoration story is beautifully told by word and picture at the small museum.

1 BLAIR ATHOLL–PITLOCHRY
9 miles (14km) 880ft (270m) OS 43 & 52

Killiecrankie Gorge

This section, between two busy tourist towns, is a relatively 'tame' walk but with a variation of moorland and wooded river valley. It includes a Forest Nature Walk and the imposing Killiecrankie Gorge. This wooded defile is best known for the battle fought near its head in 1689, won for James II (VII of Scotland) by Highlanders against the troops of King William. Some way down the gorge is the Soldier's Leap, where two rocks almost form a bridge. Here it is said a soldier made a mighty leap across the chasm to escape his closely pursuing enemies. The narrow gorge, shrouded by trees on both steep banks, is in twilight even on sunny days. It can be so forbidding that it is credible that Hessian mercenaries, fighting against Bonnie Prince Charlie in the '45 rising, refused to march through it.

SOUTH – From Blair Atholl rly station go over the level crossing just E of the station and proceed S a few yards to the river. Here a path leads in front of a row of cottages to a wooden footbridge. Cross and go S uphill past a farmhouse, through a forest and on to moorland. In 1½ miles the track forks. Take the L fork E downhill to Ardtulichan and Shelloch to a road along the River Garry. Go R on this road until near Killiecrankie it joins another road. Go L over the bridge to the village of Killiecrankie. Take the A9 S for ¼ mile to Killiecrankie Visitor Centre (worth a stop here to absorb local natural and human history and purchase pamphlets on the Nature Walks). From the Centre take the mile-long scenic path S along the river and enjoy the magnificent views. A few hundred yards short of the B8019 bridge the path crosses a footbridge to the W bank. Go L and you soon join an old road running S along the river. It passes under the B8019 and becomes a footpath which is part of a National Trust Nature Trail (did you pick up literature back at the Centre?). The Queen's View at the Linn (Pool) of Tummel is a few yards' diversion from this path. The path bears W along the Tummel for ½ mile to the Coronation Bridge. Cross here and go L on the Foss Road to Pitlochry.

Another way from the B8019 bridge is to recross the Garry by that bridge. There are steps up to it from the old road to a path (part of a Forest Walk) going down the E bank of the river to the A9 just N of Pitlochry.

NORTH – From the town centre of Pitlochry (car park and Information Centre), go R a short distance on the A9 to the road going under the rly towards the recreation ground. Follow this road to the Port na Craig suspension bridge and cross to the Foss Road. Go R to the Coronation Bridge over the Tummel, cross and go R (E) on a path along the Tummel (which at their confluence swings N along the River Garry) to the footbridge beyond the B8019. Cross here to the E bank of the Garry and go N on the path through the gorge to the Killiecrankie Visitor Centre. From here take the A9 into Killiecrankie to a road and bridge back to the W side of the river. After crossing the bridge take the first R fork to a road along the river. In ¾ mile a farm road goes L to Shelloch Farm. Here a track goes uphill and joins a track leading N down to a footbridge over the river to Blair Atholl.

rowan

2 PITLOCHRY–KIRKMICHAEL
10 miles (17km) 1150ft (350m) OS 43 & 52

The attraction of this walk lies in its passage from woods to moor and back to woods again. The movement between these contrasting environments, so closely adjoining, gives the day's experience the rhythm of a longer journey. Although we walked this on the third weekend in May, we woke to frost in Pitlochry and new snow on the mountain peaks, a wintry prospect. But as we went along the trail, the whistling of the curlews, the mouselike squeaks of the lapwings doing their acrobatics above us, and the bleating of the omnipresent young lambs, gave audible evidence of Mother Nature's confidence in a spring that would eventually catch up upon itself.

The way is easy and pleasant walking in either direction but we found that east to west was easier since that part of the trail which is on LRTs, with a steep walk down through the forest, comes at the end when you may be tiring. Also it is more aesthetically satisfying because of the view of Pitlochry to the west, with its houses and church spires nestling securely in the green valley of the Rivers Tay and Tummel. This sight, dominating half the walk and seen from the lovely open beauty of the moors, spurs you on.

EAST – From the car park in Pitlochry go S on the A9 for 1¾ miles to a road going E to Ballyoukan House. This road goes L almost immediately after the entrance to a school on the L. On the R, across the road (towards Pitlochry) is the East Haugh Hotel. (This is a farm hotel, where it would be possible to lodge if you did not want to stay in Pitlochry. It should be relatively easy to catch a bus if you wanted to avoid walking along the busy A9.) Follow the signs to Ballyoukan House. At 2 miles from Pitlochry the road divides, one branch leading over a wooden bridge to Ballyoukan House, the other going L up the hill. Take this L fork, which climbs steeply through a forest and becomes a well-defined stony LRT after it goes through gates on to the open moor. (The LRT over the moor is not marked on the map.) It continues all the way to two small bothies N of Loch Broom at 5½ miles (at 012595, a flyspeck on the OS map). The track goes NE from above Ballyoukan House and care should be taken wherever another LRT (and there are several) joins it. Check these junctions with your compass, as Loch Broom and the bothies are hidden by the shoulders of hills until you are quite close to them. From the bothies head E towards the hill in front of you. Skirt the hill to the S of it and continue E, paralleling a forest on your L, until you reach the ruins of the Mains of Glenderby. Alternatively, you can climb the hill and get a lovely view of the ruins ahead, which gives you the atmosphere of desolation typical of the Highlands today. From the hill follow the high forest fence down to the ruins. Whether climbing the hill or skirting around it, you will see the way you have to take. From the Mains of Glenderby, follow an LRT E through a young forest. This LRT takes you to the road through the chalet village of the Log Cabin Hotel. As you come among these buildings, the road divides. Take the R fork leading SE to the Croft of Cultalonie and on to the A924 at Kirkmichael.

WEST – From the centre of Kirkmichael go S off the A924 over an old stone bridge to the Croft of Cultalonie (½ mile) and R to a chalet village at Balnald. Go through the village W to an LRT up Glen Derby paralleling the Back Burn, to the Mains of Glenderby (2½ miles). From here continue parallel to the burn (no track) up the glen, crossing the Allt Bunbruach. Loch Broom will come into view to the SW. Strike for two bothies about ¾ mile N of Loch Broom (at 012595), where an LRT goes E to Ballyoukan House (8 miles) and the A9 at 8¾ miles. Pitlochry is 1¾ miles to the R.

Kirkmichael

3 KIRKMICHAEL–DUNKELD
15 miles (24km) 1310ft (400m) OS 43 & 53

lapwing

This is the most strenuous and challenging walk on this route, with 4 miles of trackless deep heather near Kirkmichael and with parts of the remainder difficult to follow. Except for the heather, the footing is good to excellent. There is no danger of remaining lost for long as the area is crossed by a number of tracks and is bounded by main roads only a few miles distant. Most of the way is over old tracks, now disused, with good footing. The north to south direction is easier, as the most difficult piece (through the heather) comes when you are fresh.

SOUTH – Leave the town centre W over an old bridge and go SW over a narrow road. In ½ mile the road forks. A faint sign on a tree by a burn points to the Croft of Cultalonie straight ahead. Go through the farmyard and the gate out on to the moor. You now have about 4 miles of rolling moorland to cover, heading SW. The going is slow through the heather and you'll find yourself watching for burnt patches and green areas to ease the walking. At about 3 miles you should strike the unnamed loch from which the Pitcarmick Burn flows (the loch has a long earth dam and boathouse with a farm building above). Go around to the head of the loch and up almost due W to a notch from which you will descend to Lochan Oisinneach Beag, where you will strike a track going S. Take care here because it is easy to go wrong. (If you go from the unnamed loch up another notch more to the S, as we first did, you will miss the lochs entirely but should strike the track at about 041538. In this case, after passing through the wrong notch, don't go back but follow the running water, first by drainage ditches, then by a stream, down to an old stone bridge where the correct track will be picked up. Don't try to strike across the heather because the correct track is heavily overgrown and may be crossed without noticing it.) From Lochan Oisinneach Beag the track goes S through the long ravine of the Buckny Burn, crosses the burn

86

on another old bridge and carries S to Riemore Lodge. It then swings W through a gate, continues for a short distance and meets the track from Loch Ordie, where you go SE to the paved road running S from Riemore Lodge. Go S on this road for about ¾ mile. Just past a stand of trees and a house made into a barn, a track goes W up past Deuchary Hill and leads over a saddle down to Mill Dam. Below the dam you will join a road coming down the W side of Mill Dam. This immediately forks and you take the R fork down the last miles, through handsome plantations and an occasional house, to the A923. Go R and then L on to the A9 to Dunkeld.

NORTH – Leave Dunkeld town centre N on the A9 then turn R on to the A923. At ½ mile a signpost 'Public Footpath to Kirkmichael 15 miles' points up an unpaved road. The road forks several times but the OS map is clear on which fork to take. At Mill Dam you pass E below the dam, up a long slant N to a bridge high above the loch. Here the road forks. Take the R fork, going E over a saddle and down to a paved road leading N (L) to Riemore Lodge. Before a bridge leading directly to the Lodge, take a track going L. In a short distance red and yellow blazes are encountered. Go about ¼ mile to a track coming in from the R and take this up the Buckny Burn. An occasional red-painted arrow will encourage you but these die out. The track is somewhat overgrown but is discernible. Take it to the head of Lochan Oisinneach Beag where you now have 4 miles of uncharted way NE across the heather to Kirkmichael. The going will be slow. There is no danger of getting lost, as you will reach one of the farms bordering the A924 at any heading from SE to NNE.

Dunkeld

BRAES of ANGUS WALK Grampians
47 miles (75km)

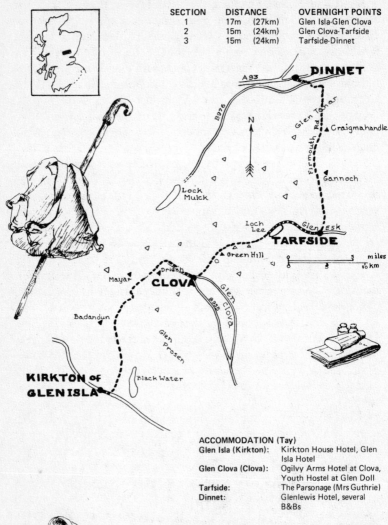

SECTION	DISTANCE		OVERNIGHT POINTS
1	17m	(27km)	Glen Isla-Glen Clova
2	15m	(24km)	Glen Clova-Tarfside
3	15m	(24km)	Tarfside-Dinnet

ACCOMMODATION (Tay)

Glen Isla (Kirkton):	Kirkton House Hotel, Glen Isla Hotel
Glen Clova (Clova):	Ogilvy Arms Hotel at Clova, Youth Hostel at Glen Doll
Tarfside:	The Parsonage (Mrs Guthrie)
Dinnet:	Glenlewis Hotel, several B&Bs

PUBLIC TRANSPORT (WAS)
Glen Isla: bus Alyth (Mon-Sat), 1 r/t daily
Glen Clova: bus Kirriemuir (Mon-Sat), 1 r/t daily
Tarfside: none
Dinnet: bus Aberdeen

The Braes of Angus, little known outside Scotland but cherished by the Scots, is the great southern slope of the Mounth, a long spine of hills between the Dee and Tay valleys. The slope is invaded by glens running up from the south and the Walk touches them all. You can truly say, when ending it, that you have walked the Angus glens – Isla, Prosen, Clova and Esk, as well as having crossed the Angus Braes. The Walk starts in Glen Isla, a well-wooded glen, goes east, touching the head of three glens, and then swings north over the Mounth by an old hill track, the Firmounth Road, to the Dee at Dinnet.

The glens are well farmed until near their heads, where they are deep in the Mounth. This is one of the charms of this area, the alternating of pastoral lowlands and high mountain moors. You have a feeling, too, of taking the easier way as you walk over the tops, since by road the route is up to four times longer. The glens are well known for their wild flowers, especially around Glen Clova. Take along your flower guide and look out for, among other things, butterwort, starry saxifrage and the mountain kingcup. Anyone staying for a longer time in the Braes can piece together other through-walks linking the glens and Deeside. The biggest problems are keeping the walks under 15 miles per day and finding accommodation.

The Walk is fairly strenuous, the sections are long and much goes over high country. There is some path-finding involved but not of a difficult sort and the footing is good. However, it is not recommended for the inexperienced.

OVERNIGHT POINTS – Kirkton of Glen Isla is a tiny village at the head of Glen Isla, the western and most heavily wooded of the glens. **Clova** is a hamlet half-way up Glen Clova, the deepest of the glens. The Youth Hostel is at the foot of Glen Doll, a small glen running from the head of Glen Clova. Above Clova the glen is hemmed in by steep mountain slopes and cliffs and is an imposing place. There are numerous day walks entailing moderately strenuous climbs followed by easy traverses across the wide high plateaus to the many mountain tops. You can bag an easy Munro or two while you are about it. The high view is as fine a panorama of peaks and lochs as any in Scotland. **Tarfside** is a small farming community in lovely Glen Esk, the most fertile of the glens. One mile east is the Glen Esk Folk Museum, which has a good exhibit of the early life of the glens (inquire locally as to opening hours). **Dinnet** is a handful of cottages, a hotel and two B&Bs on the River Dee.

1 GLEN ISLA–GLEN CLOVA
17 miles (27km) 2620ft (800m) OS 44

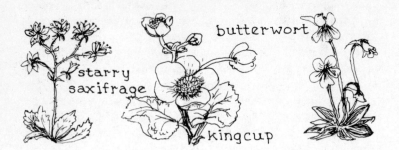

This walk is dominated at its southern end by the forest and at its northern end by the high hills surrounding Glen Clova. From Kirkton of Glen Isla it is all estate- and forest-road walking until the open hillsides of Glen Prosen. The views range from pastoral valleys and low hills geometrically patched with forests to the wide sweeps of high bare hills flanking the many small valleys which run in all directions. Part of the walk has no track but is easy to find when the visibility is good because it goes along ridges or follows narrow grassy ravines made by tiny burns. However, if the high country is in mist, it is not safe to travel the route because of the cliffs near Glen Doll. The footing is poor to excellent.

NORTH – Leave Kirkton of Glen Isla PO and walk E on the B951 to the farm road going L through East Mill Farm. Go L over a bridge and up the E side of the forest to Glen Markie Lodge (3½ miles). Behind the buildings there is a forest road going L which goes N up Glen Finlet (one L fork to be ignored). At the top of the forest the road ends in an open area and you will see a log bridge. Do not go over this bridge but go through the forest up beside the burn which the bridge spans. There is no path here, the trees crowd the burn and it is rough going for a short way until you reach the edge of the forest. Cross a stile over the forest fence and head NE for the saddle on the skyline, between Broom Hill and Craigie Thieves. There is no track but the way is easy to find in good visibility. In misty weather follow the deer fence further to your R, which will take you safely up and over the saddle. After reaching the saddle go down until you cross the larger burn which flows down Glen Prosen (8½ miles). (At this point, if the way ahead is in mist, retreat down Glen Prosen, picking up an LRT at Kilbo ruins that will take you down to Glen Prosen village).

90

Go N uphill along the ascending spine of the Shank of Drumwhallo. There is an old track here that keeps disappearing and therefore is not very useful. Go up the broad ridge of the Shank onto a high plateau and continue N until you reach a line between Mayar and Driesh. Turn E across a boulder-strewn area to a steep gully. Here the well-worn path along the slope of Drumfollow leads you down to Glen Doll (13 miles). The Ogilvy Arms at Clova is 4 miles to the R. (Glen Doll is a popular place for walkers and campers so it is fairly easy to get a lift to Clova if you feel that the last 4 miles are too much – we did!)

SOUTH – From the car park at Glen Doll take the forest path sign-posted 'Kilbo'. It is a steady climb through the forest until you come out in the open. From here you clearly see the path going up Drumfollow to the head of the ravine of the Burn of Kilbo. When you gain this you will find yourself on a wide plateau rather than a narrow ridge, with Driesh (947m) rising to the E and Mayar (928m) to the W. Go W towards the latter, cross a fence and look for a way S down the Shank of Drumwhallo. The way is not well defined but as long as you keep the deer fence on your L and descend towards the patch of forest you will be on track. As you approach the forest you will soon see that the way through shown on the OS map is no longer there as you are faced with an unbroken wall of trees. Therefore keep well to the E of the forest edge until you reach the bottom of the hill, cross a burn and carry on over the pass between the two hills on the SE skyline. There is a wee burn to follow up the hill which is sometimes hidden from the eye but never from the ear. From the saddle go down the N edge of the forest to where there is a stile. Cross it and go down a burn to a log bridge in a clearing. Here you will pick up a forest road which will take you down to Glen Markie Lodge and its estate road to Kirkton of Glen Isla.

wild iris

2 GLEN CLOVA–TARFSIDE
15 miles (24km) 2000ft (670m) OS 44

Invermark castle

This walk goes from Glen Clova, the most magnificent of the Angus glens, to Glen Esk, the most lived-in. Half of the way runs along the tops of hills and half along Glen Esk. It passes dramatic Loch Brandy, a giant mirror in a glacier-carved hanging valley rimmed by 240m cliffs. The route follows along the broad tops of three linked hills, follows the shore of steep-sided Loch Lee and then goes past a ruined castle to the farmland of Glen Esk. There is a mile or so of trackless moorland to negotiate but otherwise the way is easily followed and the footing is good to excellent.

NORTH – Behind the car park of the Ogilvy Hotel (the hotel is at the N end of the B955 loop in Glen Clova) is a signposted path to Glen Esk going NE uphill. The path is rather faint at first but becomes well worn as it climbs up to and around the SE of Loch Brandy (alas, the loch does not live up to its name!). Above the loch you will find yourself on the nearly flat summit of Green Hill (870m) the highest point on this walk. Here you will pick up cairns going E along the broad tops of Green Hill, White Hill and Muckle Cairn. The track is faint and the cairns small but the area is almost featureless and the cairns stand out. From Muckle Cairn, you head downhill across the heather for about a mile to strike an LRT (this is quite visible from Muckle Cairn). Go R on this LRT and it will lead you past the Shank of Inchgrundle to Loch Lee. (If the hilltops are in mist it is safest to go immediately downhill NE from Green Hill until you strike a burn.

The slope is safe to descend anywhere. Follow the burn down to the ruins at 372781 where a path goes along the burn to an LRT along the Water of Lee. Go R to Loch Lee.) The LRT runs along the N shore of the loch and past a ruined keep to a narrow paved road. Tarfside is 4 miles E. The Parsonage, the only accommodation in Tarfside, is behind the church W of the bridge over the Water of Tarf.

SOUTH – Go W from Tarfside by road to the head of Loch Lee and strike an LRT going up beside the Shank of Inchgrundle. Leave the LRT soon after it starts downhill beyond the Shank and head up across the heather to Muckle Cairn (bearing 230° magnetic). A line of cairns will be picked up at the top, leading first S and then W to Green Hill and the path down to Clova. (If it is misty at the top, go from Loch Lee along the Water of Lee on an LRT and L on a path up the Water of Unich to the ruins at 372781. Here follow the Burn of Slidderies (no track) and then climb Green Hill on a compass heading of 230° magnetic. Continue on this heading over and down to Clova. If the slope going down steepens alarmingly, go SE along the slope until it grows less steep – it is conceivable that you have drifted R to the cliffs of Loch Brandy. The mile-wide slope between Loch Brandy and Loch Wharral is entirely safe to descend anywhere. However, if you find yourself anxious in the mist, reverse your course (to 50° magnetic) and go back the way you came, to wait below the mist until it clears. The route back is safe anywhere. Once below the mist, check the Slidderies Burn and see, if possible, where you went wrong in your route. If the mist lifts or you find your error, you can try the hill crossing again.)

Tarfside

3 TARFSIDE–DINNET
15 miles (24km) 1870ft (570m) OS 44

wagtail   pipit

This walk follows one of the many old tracks between Deeside and the south – the Firmounth Road, running from Dinnet to Tarfside. It was used for transporting timber from the Deeside forests – hence the name 'fir' – and 'mounth' refers to the long stretch of high hills between Stonehaven and the Braemar–Blairgowrie road ('mounth' from 'monadh' or 'moine' meaning 'mountain' or 'heathy area'). Other traffic included illicit whisky, black cattle and people visiting or searching for work. The traffic dried up at the end of the eighteenth century and the road is now used only occasionally by walkers and stalkers. The way passes through a large and impressive stand of ancient Caledon pines but is mostly over high moorland. It crosses three flat-topped hills up to 720m in height. The path is well in evidence and the footing good to excellent. We walked this Mounth road from Tarfside and, as we grew weary towards the end of the day, we kept remembering the story told by Mrs Guthrie, our hostess of the night before. When she was ten her ninety-year-old grandfather announced at breakfast that he was walking to Dinnet for some grouse eggs. His daughter felt that he ought not to go alone so the young granddaughter accompanied him! A discouraging story.

NORTH – On the E side of the bridge over the Water of Tarf a farm road going N is signposted 'Aboyne by the Fungle Road'. Take this road to Shinfur (1¾ miles) (the L fork beyond the ford over the Burn of Tennet leads in ¼ mile to Shinfur.) Pass W around the farmhouse and small plantation to a moorland track. As you approach the farmhouse, you cannot fail to notice the profusion of rabbits and their warrens. We came upon 30 or 40 of them scurrying madly towards their homes in an old stone wall, as if set off on a race by a starting gun. The smaller rabbits evidently became confused in their excitement and ran repeatedly to the wrong burrow because for several minutes after all the adult rabbits had disappeared, the wall seethed with babies frantically trying to find the right home.

The track now begins to climb. At 4 miles it forks, with the L fork marked 'Firmounth Road'. Just beyond, in a line uphill, is a series of hides used for grouse shooting. The track climbs to its high point at Tampie (723m) becoming a fine gravel path for some distance over a plateau. Note the extremely short heather on each side of the path, denoting sub-Arctic conditions and warning you that the weather can be severe here. The track now dips and climbs to an almost unnoticeable saddle between Gannoch and Hill of St Colm. Here you pass 3 carved stones in the space of ½ mile, 2 incised with a large 'B', the middle one with a 12-inch circle within which are illegible letters. The track dips a second time, rising to Craigmahandle (8 miles) where it enters the Glen Tanar Nature Reserve through a gate (cairn with details of the Reserve just beyond). From here you pick up an LRT that carries you down to the bottom of Glen Tanar. It passes through several thousand acres of Caledon pines, that native tree which comprised the bulk of the ancient Caledonian Forest. Handsome in their irregular shapes, large size and wide spacing, once seen they can never be mistaken for another pine. At 12½ miles the track reaches the Braeloine Visitor Centre of the Nature Conservancy, well worth a visit. From the Centre, cross a bridge and turn R for 100yd on a paved road to a narrow road L, signposted 'Dinnet'. Follow this to the B976, go L ¼ mile to a bridge R over the Dee, with Dinnet ¼ mile beyond.

SOUTH – At the crossroads in Dinnet go S across the Dee and L on the B976 to first road on the R, which will take you down to Millfield on the Water of Tanar. From here follow the **NORTH** directions in reverse. On the track up from Millfield to the forest there are 3 side paths to the L to be avoided. They are all marked on the OS map. In Tarfside, the Parsonage is just W of the bridge over the Water of Tarf.

hawthorn

STRATHSPEY WALK Grampians
68 miles (109½km)

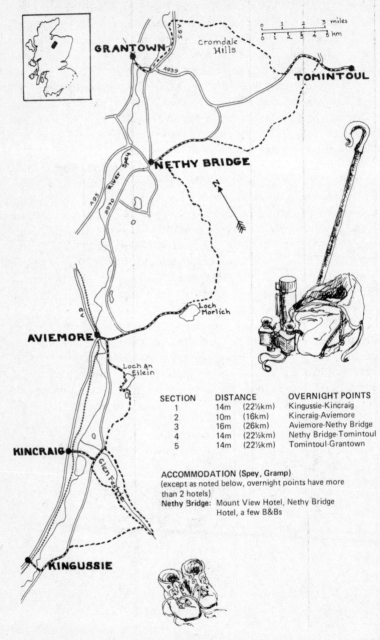

SECTION	DISTANCE		OVERNIGHT POINTS
1	14m	(22½km)	Kingussie-Kincraig
2	10m	(16km)	Kincraig-Aviemore
3	16m	(26km)	Aviemore-Nethy Bridge
4	14m	(22½km)	Nethy Bridge-Tomintoul
5	14m	(22½km)	Tomintoul-Grantown

ACCOMMODATION (Spey, Gramp)
(except as noted below, overnight points have more than 2 hotels)
Nethy Bridge: Mount View Hotel, Nethy Bridge Hotel, a few B&Bs

PUBLIC TRANSPORT (H&I)
Kingussie & Aviemore: train London, Glasgow, Edinburgh & Inverness;
bus Elgin
Kincraig & Nethy Bridge: bus Aviemore or Elgin
Tomintoul: bus Dufftown & Keith; train Keith to Aberdeen & Inverness
Grantown: bus Elgin

The route lies in Strathspey, a land of great natural beauty in the northern part of a district known as Badenoch and Strathspey. The River Spey runs through the middle, the inhabited villages and towns being mostly along or near the river. The area is bounded on the east by the Cairngorm mountains and on the west by the Monadhliath mountains.

The landscape is beautiful except where man has made it otherwise, notably on the ski slopes in the Cairngorms. The Cairngorms are the highest, and in many ways the most challenging, mountain range in the British Isles. The range does not include Britain's single highest summit (Ben Nevis, near Fort William); but it includes the next four – Ben Macdui (1309m), Braeriach (1296m), Cairn Toul (1258m) and Cairngorm (1141m). By and large the mountains lack the sharp peaks, jagged ridges and superb mixture of land and seascape found in the west. There are miles of walking above the 1000m contour. Snow can occur at any time of the year and lies continuously from November until April. The advent of the ski road and chairlift up Cairngorm has made it, in good summer weather, a gentle stroll for anyone up to the age of 100. There are a multitude of walks and scrambles and magnificent granite cliffs for rock climbing. For the long-distance walker there are three great mountain passes for walks of about 30 miles each, between Strathspey and Deeside: the Lairig Ghru, Lairig an Laoigh and Glen Feshie, a paradise in its upper reaches.

Lower down in elevation, where you will be walking, the landscape is hardly less charming. The heathery moors are a carpet of deep purple in high summer. Remnants of the ancient Caledonian forest survive in the forests of Rothiemurchus and Abernethy, filled with Scots pine, juniper and silver birch. Loch an Eilein with its nature trail is a particular jewel set in the Rothiemurchus forest. Glenmore has both remnants of the ancient forest and modern plantations, well designed and set out with forest and river trails. Lochs Alvie and Insh are other jewels.

Wildlife is abundant. Hundreds of red deer roam the high tops in summer and the glens in winter. Roe deer are found in the woods. There is a herd of reindeer, introduced from Scandinavia, in the area near Loch Morlich. Bird species include grouse, pheasant, the turkey-size capercaillzie, ptarmigan, dotterel and snow bunting, as well as eagle and buzzard. If you are lucky you may see a fox, stoat or red squirrel or even a wild cat.

The area too has all the historic associations of the Highlands. Until 1746 and the Battle of Culloden, the clan chiefs, Grant, Mackintosh and Macpherson ruled with the powers of life and death over their clan members, a sore trial to the Scottish kings. The clans fought, plundered, and stole cattle and sheep. Edward I, Hammer of the Scots, in his attempt to conquer Scotland got as far north as Lochindorb, just above Grantown. In the late fourteenth century, Alexander Stewart, Earl of Buchan, son of Robert II and known as the Wolf of Badenoch, terrorised the whole of northeast Scotland, burning Elgin Cathedral and murdering the monks. His strongholds included Lochindorb and (possibly) Loch an Eilein castles. During the seventeenth-century Civil War, James Graham, Marquis of Montrose, raised a Highland and Irish army to fight for Charles I. During 1645–46 he gained a remarkable succession of victories against the armies of the Scottish Covenanters, generally against heavy odds. After each battle most of his army went home with plunder and he had to wait, usually in the vicinity of Rothiemurchus, until they came back and he could resume the campaign. He was finally defeated, betrayed and hanged at the Grassmarket in Edinburgh. After Culloden and the destruction of the power of the clans, Strathspey, like the rest of the Highlands, suffered from the clearances, the eviction of men to make way first for sheep and then for deer. Many ruins of old crofts can be seen. With the breakup of the clan system, many of the more humane lairds attempted to improve the economic lot of their people by setting out new towns for them, such as Grantown and Tomintoul, and by introducing new industries. Lumbering in the remaining forests continued, using the Spey and its tributaries to transport the logs. The logs were rafted and run down the river by the Spey 'floaters' – men who floated the rafts downstream to Fochabers. Only the stones of the dams at the south end of Loch Morlich and the north end of Loch Eunach remain.

The Spey valley, because of its fertility, has long been the home of man, as a number of prehistoric and historic structures bear witness. None are on the Walk or near enough for a detour en route but you may be curious about them since they keep appearing on all the Ordnance Survey maps. Their names are generally given in gothic letters, as you will already have suspected since *castle* is one that frequently appears (Roman antiquities are in block letters, eg VILLA, but do not occur in the north). The most regularly occurring word may seem to be *cairn*, which means a pile of rocks marking a burial site;

but the word 'cairn' also means a pile of rocks set up by modern man. A *chambered cairn* such as that marked at 965215 on OS 36 is a burial site that had a chamber constructed for the body, rather than just having the stones heaped over it. *Standing stones*, such as those noted on the bank of the Spey 1 mile east of Dulnain Bridge are obvious in form but their function is still debated. A *souterrain*, such as that noted at 776019, OS 36, 2 miles north of Kingussie, is an underground house. A *settlement*, such as the one 1 mile northeast of Loch an Eilein, is a village, defended somewhat less formidably than a *fort* or *dun*. Almost all prehistoric structures are a disappointment to visit, we find, since the visible evidence of their existence is often slight and they are, at best, in a highly ruinous state. You need a discerning eye and keen imagination to re-create the original. (If you are further interested, Rachael Feachem's *Guide to Prehistoric Scotland* (Batsford, 1977), gives an extensive list, with locations and descriptions of a variety of sites.) Thus the Spey valley is a record both of ancient and modern man and, as it sweeps north, carved by its river, it is a mirror of local history.

OVERNIGHT POINTS – Kingussie, planned as a woollen centre in the eighteenth century, is a popular tourist centre. It has the Highland Folk Museum which contains interesting exhibits on early Highland life. Across the Spey is the ruined Ruthven Barracks, built in 1716 to help maintain order in the Highlands and destroyed by Highlanders in the last abortive rising, of 1745. **Kincraig** is an attractive small village near Loch Insh. Two miles south is the Highland Wildlife Park which, while mainly a drive-through park, has a small exhibition area for pedestrians. There are boats for hire and instruction in sailing on Loch Insh and the nearby Insh Marsh's Nature Reserve is a bird sanctuary worth visiting, not to be confused with the better-known osprey sanctuary at Loch Garten. **Aviemore** is a well-developed walking, climbing and skiing centre. It is a busy place in all seasons, with hotels, shops, a cinema, etc. **Nethy Bridge** is a small village on the River Nethy. Abernethy Church and the ruined Castle Roy are nearby. **Tomintoul,** the loftiest village in the Highlands (350m), is a planned town founded in 1779. **Grantown** is a sizeable town on the River Spey, planned and founded in 1765 and built largely of granite. It is an excellent centre for fishing on the Spey.

heather

1 KINGUSSIE–KINCRAIG
14 miles (22½km) 340ft (105m) OS 35

remnant of the Caledonian forest

This walk is a mixture of quiet roads, moorland and forest, running partly along Glen Feshie. You get splendid views of the Glen and the Sgorans range, which are magnificent and well worth further exploration. The footing is nearly all good, the way easy to find, with only a very short section without a path.

NORTHEAST – Opposite the Duke of Gordon Hotel in Kingussie, go S on a minor road past the rly station and school and across the River Spey until you reach the junction with the B970. Turn L (the ruins of Ruthven Barracks will be on your L) and in 2 miles you will come to Tromie Bridge, across which you turn L again. A short distance brings you to the road turning off to the R to Drumguish. Follow this and at a cluster of houses reached in ½ mile carry straight on by the public footpath to Glen Feshie. The path crosses a moorland and enters a plantation. Ignore any diversions L or R. About 2 miles inside the plantation, the track swings round by a couple of hairpin turns and brings you out by the Allt Chomhraig. Very soon, you cross a footbridge opposite the abandoned croft of Baileguish. Here the track peters out and you go E across moorland (with luck finding another footbridge across a tributary) towards an old Nissen hut surrounded by a dyke (Corarnstilmore). Here the track reappears, following more or less a line of telegraph poles and leading you into another plantation.

Another mile or so brings you out on a private road overlooking the River Feshie, with the still inhabited croft of Achlean opposite you on the other side of the river. Go R for ¾ mile to a footbridge over the Feshie. Cross and turn L (N) along the E bank of the Feshie, past the abandoned cottage of Achleum and over a stile to Achlean. Here you walk 5 miles along a quiet road going N, past a glider field and Lagganlea (an outdoor centre) until you come out on the B970 at Feshiebridge. Turn L, down the hill, cross the bridge and go R on first road through the grounds of Invereshie House to the road to Kincraig (R).

SOUTHWEST – From Kincraig cross the River Spey, go L on public footpath to the B970 and L to Feshiebridge (1½ miles). Take the side road to Lagganlea up the hill just after the bridge over the River Feshie and continue S to Achlean. Here a path goes between two cottages past Achleum. ¾ mile from Achlean is a footbridge over the Feshie. Cross and go N until opposite Achlean, where a track goes L through a plantation. At the edge of the plantation the track disappears and you must work your way W to Baileguish, cross the Allt Chomhraig on a bridge to a track going W to the B970 at Drumguish. Go L on the B970 to Ruthven and the road to Kingussie.

DIVERSIONS – Going NE, where the track from Drumguish reaches Glen Feshie, you can take the road along the W bank of the Feshie to the B970 at Insh House and N to Kincraig Road. At Ballintean on this W bank road, you can diverge again, by a footpath along the W bank of the Feshie that brings you into Feshiebridge. Either diversion will save about 1½ miles.

Ruthven barracks

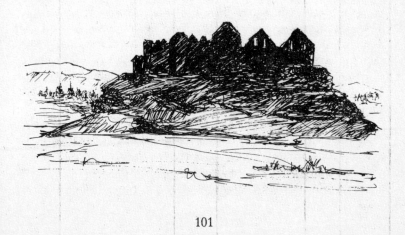

2 KINCRAIG–AVIEMORE
10 miles (16km) 290ft (88m) OS 35 & 36

Feshiebridge

This is an easy walk from quiet Kincraig to busy Aviemore, by Loch Insh, across Inshriach Forest and around that jewel of Strathspey, Loch an Eilein (Loch of the Island). It is mostly by forest roads, with many glimpses of the Cairngorm tops. The footing is generally good to excellent, the way clear underfoot but slightly bewildering in the Forest because of the multiplicity of forest roads.

NORTHEAST – Leave Kincraig and walk SE past Loch Insh to the B970 and go N to Feshiebridge (1½ miles). Cross the bridge over the Feshie River and continue by road, swinging L and ascending slightly until you reach the R turn for Achlean. Follow this for a very short distance until you see a forest gate to your L. Now you have to find your way through the forest of the Moor of Feshie. The forest roads shown in the OS maps are there but so are others. The following directions should get you through. Starting from the gate off the Achlean road, go through the forest to the first intersection, which comes in about 7min and offers 3 tracks of which the correct one is that to the L. The next intersection, after another 15min, again offers 3 tracks of which the correct one is that to the R. After yet another 15min, the third intersection offers 2 tracks: the correct one is that to the R. At all 3 of these points the correct track is the broadest and newest-looking one. Finally after walking for a total of 45min or so from the Achlean road, for the first time you take a minor track going off R from the main track. In 30yd or so this brings you to a stile over a deer fence at the edge of the forest. You will know if you are on the

102

right track if, the day being clear, you see a humpy hill with a large rock clearly visible on the skyline. This rock is the Argyll Stone, so called because here in 1594 the Earl of Argyll took refuge in order to avoid the hostile attentions of the pursuing Earl of Huntly after the battle of Glenlivet. You will know you are at the right stile if immediately beyond it you see the Cairngorm Nature Reserve sign.

Choosing the wrong track will either bring you to a dead end among the trees, in which case you patiently go back to the previous intersection and try again; or lead you prematurely out on to the B970, in which case make the best of a bad job by continuing north to Aviemore, diverting, if you like, to Loch an Eilein at the signposted road thereto. If you get fed up with being lost and turn E through the trees you will come to a deer fence, which you will have to climb. Beyond the fence you should turn N and follow the edge of the plantation, either picking up the track at the stile or, if beyond it, coming finally to Loch Gamhna and carrying on from there.

Assuming you do find the Nature Reserve sign, turn L (N) following a somewhat obscure path which bends E away from the forest until you see, on a pleasant grass plot among the trees to the R, Inshriach bothy where you can have a rest. Then carry on N. Soon after leaving the bothy, the path crosses a burn and becomes a bit obscure but if you lose it don't worry. You are bound, before very long, to see both Loch Gamhna and Loch an Eilein.

Having reached the point at which the burn flows out of Loch Gamhna and into Loch an Eilein, you can go around the latter on the Nature Trail, going either way to the car park. From the car park a road goes to the B970 where you turn R to Inverdruie and Aviemore, or in a few yards you can take a track going R to a road past Black Park Cottage and on to Inverdruie and Aviemore.

SOUTHWEST – Go E from Aviemore to the B970 and S to Doune to a road going L to Loch an Eilein. Go S round the loch to the E side of Loch Gamhna where a faint track goes S to a plantation and bothy. Go E to a stile over a deer fence to a forest track. To get from here to Kincraig, carefully study the **NORTHEAST** directions, reversing them.

gorse

3 AVIEMORE–NETHY BRIDGE
16 miles (26km) 590ft (180m) OS 36

An Lochan Uaine

This is an agreeable walk with interesting diversions. It moves from the busy holiday town of Aviemore to quiet Nethy Bridge, by woodlands and moors under the north edge of the great Cairngorm range. There are frequent views of the tops to the south, especially the superb massif of Braeriach with its northern corries. There is an opportunity to climb an outlying mountain, if you so desire. The footing is fair to excellent, the path-finding not difficult. A bus or taxi between Aviemore and Glen More will reduce the walk to 10 miles.

NORTH – Walk S on the A9 from the Aviemore rly station for ½ mile to the A951. Go E on the A951 to Coylumbridge (2 miles) and take the road to Loch Morlich and Glen More. There will be frequent views of the Cairngorm range. At 5 miles you will reach Loch Morlich and in another mile Glen More. Take the road to Glenmore Lodge where, at 7 miles, it becomes a forest track going NE and N up the narrow valley of the (mostly invisible) Allt na Feith Duibhe. At 8 miles you will find the An Lochan Uaine (the green loch). This is a beautiful spot to halt for lunch, where you can admire the remarkable greenness of the dark waters and ponder the enigma that no burn flows into or out of the loch. Shortly beyond the loch the track divides. Take the L fork, to Ryvoan bothy (9 miles) and continue straight ahead for another 2 miles. Just where the track seems to go through a gate, you bear L towards the buildings of the abandoned Rynettin croft. From here go downhill and in a mile come to Forest Lodge, a mock-Tudor mansion. Turn sharp L out of the lodge grounds and in less than a mile turn sharp R down a forest track, not worrying about it being marked 'Private'. This will eventually bring you to the centre of Nethy Bridge.

SOUTH – From Nethy Bridge Hotel walk S on the B970 across the bridge over the Nethy and turn L in front of the grocer's shop past some houses and the church. Soon the road bears S. Ignore any side roads and in about a mile the road becomes a forest track marked 'Private'. At its end turn L and you will come to the entrance to Forest Lodge. Just inside the gate turn sharp R and walk up to Rynettin croft. Beyond, the track bears around to the L and joins a forest track at which you turn R (S), Bynack More's cone being clearly visible to the SE. Continue on past Ryvoan bothy, An Lochan Uaine and Glenmore Lodge to the motor road. Aviemore is 6 miles to the W.

DIVERSIONS – (a) Since we recommend the bus between Aviemore and Glen More to avoid walking on a very busy road, you save 6 miles. You may wish to utilise the energy saved in a climb up Meall a Bhuchaille for the magnificent views it affords. This adds about 400m in elevation and about 1½hr in time but very little distance. Coming from Aviemore, start from the Forestry Commission Information Centre and take the track going L (N) through a plantation. The track is a bit obscure and wet in places but provided you keep 'between' as distinct from 'among' the trees, you should in ½hr emerge from the trees at a deer fence and stile. Beyond you will pick up small green-and-white posts leading to the col between Creagan Gorm on the L and the Bhuchaille on the R. At the col turn R (E) and follow a fairly clear track with occasional posts to the summit cairn where the view will reward your climb (your map and compass will help identify the profusion of peaks). From here a line of posts NE will guide you by a track down to Ryvoan bothy. Reverse these directions coming from Nethy Bridge. The posts are easy to pick up at the bothy. (b) There is a pleasant 6-mile diversion that avoids 4 miles of the motor road between Coylumbridge and Glen More. Go up the Lairig Ghru track, which starts just before the caravan park at Coylumbridge. About 1 mile past the Cairngorm Club Footbridge (see OS map) is an intersection known unofficially as Piccadilly. Go straight across this intersection and in less than 1 mile you will strike an LRT. Go L to Loch Morlich.

red grouse

105

4 NETHY BRIDGE–TOMINTOUL
14 miles (22½km) 840ft (260km) OS 36

This is a 'wildlife' walk as there is a good chance of seeing roe deer, pheasant and capercaillzie in the forest; and grouse, mountain hare and possibly red deer on the moorland. The grouse are particularly in evidence near Dorback Lodge, their shrill cry, sounding like an irritated 'go back, go back', being unmistakable. In reasonable weather you will also have good views of the Cairngorms and the other hills round about. The walk is half on quiet tarmac roads in attractive country and half on moorland. The footing is good to excellent, the way not difficult to find except that forest roads are proliferating so rapidly that your map and this narrative may well be out of date by the time you reach the area. It may, therefore, be useful to read the section on Route Finding – see page 172.

EAST – From the Nethy Bridge Hotel walk S for a few yards. Just before the bridge over the Nethy, turn L (E) along the Tomintoul road. Go straight ahead for 1 mile to the second junction, turn R and walk about 2 miles to a turnoff to the R, signposted 'Dorback 2¾ miles'. Take this turning, a pleasant lane past cottages and an old schoolhouse, climbing gradually through more open moor. After you arrive at the gate of Dorback Lodge, take the track to the L of the gate. Sight and sound should tell you that the land on the L is grouse moor (used by the Lodge for shooting). Here there is a profusion of heathers, of rich colours in the summer. You see the Lodge and some cottages on the R as you continue a gradual ascent. About a mile beyond the Lodge you will pass, slightly up the hill on the R, a former croft house (Fae) now renovated. A little beyond this point, just through a gate, the track forks. Take the R fork, ascending the hill and shortly passing, to your R, an abandoned croft, Letteraiten. Another mile or so, during which the path begins to descend, brings you to the Burn of Brown. Cross and turn L (N) in front of a plantation. Just after the end of the plantation, watch for an iron gate on the R, with a slightly obscure track winding up the hill beyond it. Go through the gate and follow the track which soon becomes clearer. Ignore one or two apparent diversions to the L. You will see several abandoned crofts. When you have passed close by one ruined croft house on your L you will see ahead another plantation into which the track leads. Enter through a gate and a mile or so through the trees will bring you past an imposing mansion, Kylnadrochit Lodge, on your R. Continue on until you come out on to the A939 at Bridge of Avon. Go R on the A939 1½ miles to Tomintoul.

WEST – Walk N from Tomintoul on the A939 for 1½ miles to the junction with the B9136 at Bridge of Avon. Cross the bridge, go past the traffic lights up the hill and in about 50yd find a driveway to Kylnadrochit Lodge on the L. Follow this driveway past the Lodge gates to a track ascending through a plantation and then over open moorland with ruined crofts visible on the R, down to the Burn of Brown. Go L between the burn and a plantation. Near the end of the plantation cross the burn to another track, which ascends steeply W at first, then descends gently. 1½ miles from the burn the abandoned croft house of Letteraiten appears on your L. When you come to a gate on your L, go through it and past the renovated croft house of Fae. In another mile you pass Dorback Lodge and some cottages on your L before reaching a tarmac road. Follow this for 2¾ miles to a junction and turn L. Nethy Bridge is 3 miles ahead.

DIVERSION – The 5¾ miles of road between Nethy Bridge and Dorback Lodge can be avoided by a diversion that adds 3 miles to the walk. From Nethy Bridge follow the route to Aviemore as far as Forest Lodge. Go E and then S around the Lodge, pass S of Carn a Chnuic, N of Loch a Chnuic and E through the notch of Eag Mhor to the Dorback Lodge road at Ballintuim. It is a tricky bit of route-finding through interesting country, particularly the stony defile of Eag Mhor, an ideal place for an ambush.

roe deer

5 TOMINTOUL–GRANTOWN
14 miles (22½ km) 1570ft (480m) OS 36

This is a worthwhile walk over the Hills of Cromdale, with splendid views in all directions on a fine day. It is a bit strenuous, requiring some tramping in thick heather if you go wrong. The footing is excellent to poor, the way clear to invisible, with a 3-mile pathless trek over the Hills of Cromdale. The walk can begin or end at the small village of Cromdale, 3 miles from Grantown (only one source of accommodation, the pleasant Haugh Hotel), or be broken there, if using the **NORTHWEST** direction, by an early dinner before going on to Grantown for the night, or by staying overnight and walking into Grantown the next morning.

NORTHWEST – Walk N out of Tomintoul for 4½ miles on the A939 to Bridge of Brown. About ¼ mile beyond the bridge, turn R up the road to Mains of Glenlochy Farm. Just before the farm buildings take a path bearing L to Lyntelloch, an abandoned cottage with outbuildings. Just past Lyntelloch the slight problems of this section begin. The path marked on the 1-inch OS map (none now marked on the new series) crossing the March Burn and then continuing up the N bank of the burn was a figment of the Ordnance Survey's imagination. The best route is of course the one we did not take because we went looking for the nonexistent path. We recommend that between Lyntelloch and some ruins, before you reach the burn, bear L up towards the col between Carn Tuairneir, a long rounded hump on the L, and Creagan a'Chaise, a more pronounced hump with a visible cairn, on the R. In other words, keep on the S bank of the burn 20–30m above it. This way at least you will be walking mostly over rough grass, rather than ploughing through the thick and tiring heather on the N side of the burn. Having reached the col, about 7½ miles from Tomintoul, it is well worth turning NE and scrambling over the boulders to the summit of Creagan a'Chaise (722m). You could even leave your knapsack at the col and come back for it without serious risk of theft. Assuming you go to the summit carrying your luggage, head for a smaller cairn on a lower hump to the NW. From here, or from the col, if it is a clear day, you will see the rest of the route to Cromdale. If it is misty, proceed on a magnetic bearing of about 330° from the col or Creagan a'Chaise. Head towards a little round hillock marked as a plantation on the map, centred roughly at grid reference 087269 (see 'Incidence of Adjoining Sheets and National Grid Reference System' on the right-hand side of map for an explanation of grid reference numbers). Before reaching it you will cross an expanse of wet ground on the Haughs of Cromdale. It does not matter which way you go round the hillock (now felled scrub with a few trees). We went L, clockwise, passing ruins and swinging round R, with the Glenlivet distillery and its sweet aroma on our L. Soon you come to the well-equipped farm of Lethendry with its fine cattle herd. Go through the farmyard, past the house and down a minor road. Here turn L and in ¾ mile you will arrive at Cromdale by the Haugh Hotel on the A95.

Having dined or breakfasted as the case may be, go S on the A95 to the first turn on the R, down past Cromdale Church to the Spey. Across the bridge the road turns R and then bears L. You can cut this corner by going across a field. Another ½ mile or so brings you to the B9102. Go L for 1½ miles to Grantown.

SOUTHEAST – Go N on the A939 to the B9102 then R for 1½ miles to a road leading across the Spey to Cromdale and the A95. Go N several hundred yards over the bridge and R on a minor road for ¾ mile to the turnoff for Lethendry. Pass on either side of a small hill and head across the moor (no path) to a col between Creagan a'Chaise and Carn Tuairneir (compass heading 150° magnetic). From the col you go down the S bank of the March Burn to Tomlay, Mains of Glenlochy and Bridge of Brown. Tomintoul is 4½ miles to the L on the A939.

Cults

GLENSHIEL WALK N.W. Highlands
44½ miles (72km)

SECTION	DISTANCE		OVERNIGHT POINTS
1	12m	(19km)	Tomdoun-Cluanie Bridge
2	7m	(11km)	Cluanie Bridge-Glen Affric
3	12½m	(20km)	Glen Affric-Shiel Bridge
4	13m	(21km)	Shiel Bridge-Glenelg

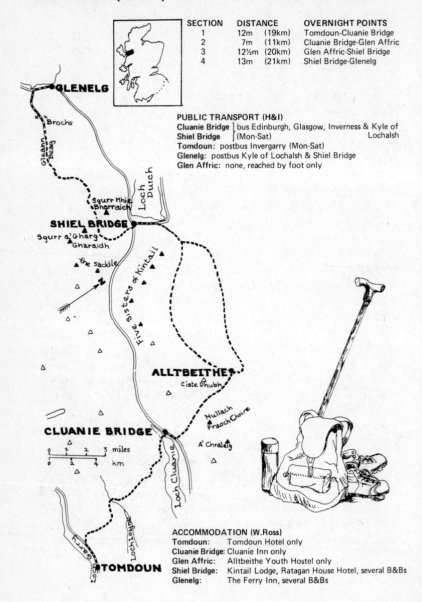

PUBLIC TRANSPORT (H&I)
Cluanie Bridge ⎫ bus Edinburgh, Glasgow, Inverness & Kyle of
Shiel Bridge ⎰ (Mon-Sat)   Lochalsh
Tomdoun: postbus Invergarry (Mon-Sat)
Glenelg: postbus Kyle of Lochalsh & Shiel Bridge
Glen Affric: none, reached by foot only

ACCOMMODATION (W.Ross)
Tomdoun: Tomdoun Hotel only
Cluanie Bridge: Cluanie Inn only
Glen Affric: Alltbeithe Youth Hostel only
Shiel Bridge: Kintail Lodge, Ratagan House Hotel, several B&Bs
Glenelg: The Ferry Inn, several B&Bs

One of the most interesting of our Walks in Scotland is from the heart of Glen Garry to the west coast near Skye. The way winds entirely through mountain wilderness, crossing high ridges and passes, going through deep narrow valleys and past great lochs. It includes one night in the truly remote Glen Affric Youth Hostel, accessible only by foot, a walk past two of the best-preserved brochs (those strange bottle-shaped fortified dwellings found only in Scotland), and some of the finest mountain scenery in Britain. This Walk shares a feature of the Central Highland Walk in that one of its stopping points is an old inn (Cluanie Inn), which sits by itself along a popular upgraded motor route with the next nearest lodging miles away. The fact that for the walker it is the *only* place to stay, whereas for the motorist it can be just a building noticed as he whizzes by, accentuates the time dichotomy between walking and driving through this country. Much of the way is easy to follow but there are a few trackless bits not too difficult to negotiate. The footing is fair to excellent. It is possible to connect from Shiel Bridge by bus with the Dornie–Achnashellach Route at Dornie.

OVERNIGHT POINTS – **Tomdoun** is the pleasant angler's hotel situated where the western end of Loch Garry merges with Loch Poulary, in the lonely grandeur of the mountainous Knoydart district. **Cluanie Bridge** is no more than an old bridge over the western end of Loch Cluanie on the former route between Glengarry and the west coast. Nearby is the old Cluanie Inn (modernised in 1979). The locale is visually stunning, with mountains rising steeply in every direction except for the precipitous valley of Loch Cluanie. **Alltbeithe** is the single building of a Scottish Youth Hostel (open only June, July and August; see Public Transport and Accommodation, page 168), in the upper part of Glen Affric, accessible only by foot. For the feeling of sheer solitude it cannot be equalled. **Shiel Bridge** is a scattered community around the head of Loch Duich, a grand fjord-like sea loch. The loch is enclosed by high hills and mountains, the most notable being the Five Sisters of Kintail, dominated by Sgurr Fhuaran. **Glenelg** is a hamlet on the Sound of Sleat, facing the Isle of Skye. On the edge of the hamlet are the ruins of Bernera Barracks, built in 1722 with soldiers quartered until 1790. It is worth a short visit. The site of Gavin Maxwell's *Ring of Bright Water* is nearby at Sandaig.

1 TOMDOUN–CLUANIE BRIDGE
12 miles (19km) 1150ft (350m) OS 33 & 34

start for Cluanie

This is a lonely walk over two mountain ridges and across a deserted valley, from Glen Garry to Loch Cluanie. It is entirely in open country, with constant views of mountains and lochs. The way is by old hill tracks and an abandoned motor road. The footing is fair to excellent. Except for a short easily negotiated stretch, the way is clearly visible.

NORTH – From the Tomdoun Hotel go W 3 miles on the motor road to a bridge over the Allt a'Ghobhainn (Burn of the Blacksmith). Just E of the bridge a track goes NW on the E side of the burn, turning due N in ½ mile and climbing to a saddle (track forks before the saddle, take the L fork), then descends NW into the long valley of the Loyne River. The track at first is clear underfoot, easily followed and generally dry. There is a good view back into Glen Garry from the saddle. When the bottom of the Loyne valley is reached, the track swings W, grows boggy and indistinct. Since the river must be forded it is the walker's choice where to cross. You can go straight across the valley from the lower part of the descending trail or go W for a while before crossing. Once across the valley there is a track running E–W along the 250m contour. Go E on this track to Allt a'Giubhais (ruins in sight just beyond). There is a very old path along the burn, its age and presence attested by the lichen-covered cairns along it, but this path need not be found as the hillside can be ascended anywhere. Go up the hill to the old motor road running L to Cluanie Bridge. An alternative way of crossing the valley is to go much further W along the S side of the river, crossing to the E–W track on the N side of the river and going W until a track is reached leading uphill to the R between Creag Mhaim and Creag Liathtais, meeting the old motor road 100yd from the substantial stone bridge where the first way comes in. The road you are now on was once part of the motor road from Invergarry to Kyle of Lochalsh, abandoned when the damming of Loch Loyne flooded part of the route. Cluanie Bridge and Cluanie Inn are 4¾ miles to the L.

SOUTH – From Cluanie Inn go E on the A87 200yd to the old road going R over Cluanie Bridge (note foundations of an earlier bridge). In 1 mile branch R over a locked gate. The road climbs to and crosses a wide plateau. Just as the road swings E it crosses a large stone bridge. Here you will leave the road to go down to the Loyne valley by either of two ways, but before you do, look S across the valley (exactly S from the stone bridge) and you will see a notch on the far ridge. This is a pass through which you will later go. It is not visible from the valley floor so keep its approximate position in mind. The alternative ways are: (a) a few yards before the bridge, an easily seen track goes uphill SW between Creag Mhaim and Creag Liathtais and down to a track along the N side of the River Loyne. Go E along this track by the river to a ford; or (b) from the bridge follow down the W side of the burn, by a faint track (which is picked up in 100yd), to the same E–W track on the N side of the River Loyne. Go W on this track and leave it to cross the river wherever you find a shallow spot, turning E on a faint track along the far side of the river. This swings uphill roughly opposite the stone bridge you just left and becomes a clear track up through the pass and down to the narrow motor road in Glen Garry. The Tomdoun Hotel is 3 miles to the L. A note on fording the River Loyne: the river is normally less than 6in deep at the riffles, does not have much current, and can be safely and easily crossed at such points. However, if it is swollen with rain (in spate), go W along the bank until it grows shallow enough to cross. This may add a mile or two to your journey.

2 CLUANIE BRIDGE–GLEN AFFRIC
7 miles (11km) 650ft (200m) OS 33

This is the short route to the most remote Youth Hostel in Britain, Alltbeithe, at the head of Glen Affric. It leads from Loch Cluanie by the narrow An Caorann Mor Valley to the head of Glen Affric. Three Munros line the way (peaks over 914m): Ciste Dhubh (982m) on the W; Mullach Fraoch Choire (1102m) and A'Chralaig (1120m) on the E. Whether you walk into or out of the head of Glen Affric, you will be impressed with the majesty of the mountains which flank the glens through which you tread. The rock cliffs of Ciste Dhubh are especially noteworthy. Walking up from Cluanie, you have the feeling of penetrating a locked mountain fastness. It would be almost impossible to lose the way as the valley runs in a straight north-to-south direction enclosed by the mountains, with no tempting way out until you reach the wide valley of Glen Affric. The footing is poor to good, with a considerable amount of boggy ground.

Alltbeithe, because of its remoteness, is limited in its amenities – while Calor Gas is provided for cooking, washing yourself and the dishes is done in the burn. No indoor plumbing is available and, if hostel users wish to be warm, a sign directs them to the peat hags for supplies of wood. We thought this latter a joke but found the stumps and roots of the original Caledonian forest exposed wherever erosion had worn a channel through the peat. It is thought-provoking to watch a fire from wood that grew so long ago as to be buried under a foot of peat. Was it bronze or iron that cut the trees?

We were amused by another sign inside the door of the hostel: 'the Ritz we ain't but take off your boots'. As we did so we mused on how much more exclusive than the Ritz the hostel is, since the only way to get there is to walk on your own two legs carrying on your back your basic necessities. The hostel, however, on a relative scale for that area, merits not one star but two. One star would go to the Camban bothy 2 miles to the west, with hardly more than four walls and a roof. Although we shared our night's shelter with only one other walker, we felt the comradely spirit of that host of walkers who came before us, from the experienced climber to the footsore novice.

NORTH – Walk E from Cluanie Inn on the A87 for 1 mile, past a forest on your R. 200yd beyond the bridge over the Allt a'Chaorainn Mhoir, opposite a group of farm buildings, an LRT goes L up the valley (paved for the first 100yd), becoming rougher and stonier as you progress. This ends at a shieling and you take a hill track N, which disappears and reappears, depending on the wetness of the ground.

There are cairns along the track but a sharp eye is needed to find the next low cairn ahead which marks a bit of track over firm ground. We found ourselves losing sight of them as we addressed ourselves to the more pressing task of finding the driest spot to put our feet. Staying on the path is not important except for being quicker and more efficient in getting over the terrain. Of course, there is your pride in path-finding. The part which is most clearly cairned is where the steep E slope of Coire a'Ghlas-thuill comes closest to the burn, but even here it is possible to walk along further up the slope. As you approach Glen Affric where your burn joins the River Affric, you will find the footing drier if you follow a contour line around the N shoulder of Mullach, descending only when opposite the bridge over the river leading to the hostel. You can also slog along the S bank of the river as the map suggests.

SOUTH – From the hostel, cross the bridge over the River Affric and pick up a track either along the river or higher up the slope of Mullach, turning S down into An Caorann Mor valley well before the Allt a'Chomhlain. Ciste Dhubh will be on your R and Mullach on your L as you traverse ground alternately boggy and heathery. At the scree slope under A'Chralaig the track becomes a rocky LRT going down to the A87 1 mile E of Cluanie Inn.

Alltbeithe

3 GLEN AFFRIC–SHIEL BRIDGE
12½ miles (20km) 1670ft (510m) OS 33

Loch a'Bhealaich

This walk passes through magnificent mountain glens, from the remote Youth Hostel at Alltbeithe in Glen Affric to the fjord-like Loch Duich. There are two routes, one by Gleann Lichd and the other by Gleann Choinneachain and Loch a Bhealaich. Both are interesting, but the latter is recommended for having more variety of landscape. Both routes are by well-trodden paths through deep valleys so it would be difficult to go astray. The footing is poor to good, the distances about the same.

WEST – Go W from Alltbeithe Youth Hostel along the River Affric and cross the footbridge over the Allt Beithe Garbh (first bridge). Go R up the W bank of this burn on a well-worn footpath, which will swing W after a gentle climb and run parallel to the Allt Gleann Gniomhaidh. In grassy areas the path will disappear, to reappear on firmer ground beyond. In places the original path is sufficiently in evidence to show that it had been carefully made, probably as a stalker's path before the turn of the century. It is too narrow for farm wagons and too well made for walking so we assumed it to be a track for stalkers' horses. The path leaves Gleann Gniomhaidh by a low pass (3½ miles) and descends to the sandy S shore of Loch a Bhealaich (good for a swim on a hot day). Beyond the loch the path ascends across the E slope of Meall a Bhealaich and zig-zags up and over the Bealach an Sgairne (5 miles). Ahead of you is the steep narrow Gleann Choinneachain. The upper part of this glen is a jumble of rocks but it soon turns into a steep grassy V with the burn running in a narrow gorge at the bottom and with the cliffs above soaring to the skyline.

The path clings to the S and W slopes of Buidhe Bheinn until you reach Strath Croe. In the strath the way is through meadows until Innis a Chrotha. From here a paved road carries you to Morvich (10 miles). The National Trust Information Office here is well worth a visit. You shortly reach the old road leading round the head of Loch Duich. Shiel Bridge is 1 mile to the L, on the A87. Part of the A87 can be avoided by following the old road near Kintail Lodge, marked as a footpath to Shiel Bridge. B&Bs are scattered around the head of Loch Duich, from Inverinate round to Ratagan.

EAST – Go N on the A87 to the old road around the head of Loch Duich and on to Morvich. From Morvich take the road going past the Highland Region Activities Centre and just over a small bridge go R a few yards to a turf-capped stone wall. On its E side a path, signposted 'Falls of Glomach', goes L. Near Dorusduain take the R fork (the L fork goes to the Falls). From here follow the **WEST** directions in reverse.

ALTERNATIVE – From Alltbeithe follow the River Affric up Eionngleann on a well-worn path on the W side of the river, over a pass into Gleann Lichd. You will soon pass the Camban bothy, which was rebuilt as a memorial to Philip Trantor, a well-loved mountaineer. It is a snug stone cottage with a sleeping loft. When we passed by, we found that its transient guests had left it clean and tidy, the only signs of their occupancy being the small plastic bags of odds and ends of food hung from the rafters on nails to keep them safe from mice. Our son took pleasure in examining their varied contents as well as perusing the entries in the bothy book, to which he added his own 'deathless prose'. The scenery in the mile before you reach Glenlicht House (now belonging to the University of Edinburgh Mountaineering Club) is particularly impressive, as the path winds down the side of a gorge past several waterfalls. Just before Glenlicht House, 2 suspension bridges span the River Croe and its tributary. The second bridge is ¼ mile W, further upstream, and is not in sight of the first. From Glenlicht House the way is by a rocky LRT which runs down the glen to Morvich. When doing the walk in the opposite direction, there is a sign to Gleann Lichd ¼ mile E of Morvich, just before the Highland Region Activities Centre.

4 SHIEL BRIDGE–GLENELG
13 miles (21km) 1500ft (460m) OS 33

Interesting in the variety of landscapes and footing, this is one of our most beautiful walks. It moves from one narrow sea loch to another, along wooded roads, by ancient monuments, across open mountain meadows and over a high rocky pass, with constantly changing views of mountain peaks. Two of the four best-preserved brochs in Britain, and the ruins of an even older Iron Age dun or fort, are encountered. The walk is moderately strenuous and requires a bit of path-finding at the halfway stage.

WEST – From the caravan park just off the A87 on the old road to Glenshiel Lodge, a path leads up the E side of the Allt Undalain, crosses a wooden bridge and climbs gently up the Undalain valley. Towards the head of the valley the path turns W steeply up and around the shoulder of Sgurr Mhic Bharraich. Do not be drawn away during the ascent by a well-worn track to the L but keep going steeply up the shoulder until reaching the Loch Coire nan Crogachan. Ahead there is a rocky ravine framing distant green pastures and the far Cuillins of Skye. The path goes downhill past a waterfall on the R and through the ravine. When the Glenmore River comes into view below, the path descends steeply to a moor. To the R in the distance you will see a small building, named Bealachasan on the map, and a wide slash in the forest just beyond it. Head directly for this house as the path across the moor is hard to find and the moorland is good walking anywhere. At Bealachasan cross the burn, go through a forest gate and turn L downhill along the fence for several hundred yards to a forestry road along the forest edge. Follow this until you see a bridge on your L, over the Glenmore River. Cross this bridge, turn R along the river for a short distance and then head W. In ¼ mile you will reach a large walled enclosure. Go L and follow along the wall to the small farm building at its W end, marked Suardalan. A track passes 100yd W of this building, faint here but more marked later on. It goes S uphill to the W of Torr Beag, a volcanic hump of some height. The track steadily improves, becoming first a good LRT and then a paved road at Balvraid. This will carry you down to the coastal road. Glenelg is 1¼ miles to the R.

EAST – From Glenelg, go S on the paved road along the shore of Glenelg Bay and the Sound of Sleat and in 1¼ miles turn E up the Gleann Beag road (signposted to the brochs). At 3¼ miles you will pass between the two brochs. Beyond Balvraid (4¼ miles), the motor road ends and a good LRT is met. The ruins of an Iron Age fort, Dun

Grugaig, come into view shortly, perched to the right on a knoll high above Abhainn a'Ghlinne Bhig (Burn of the Little Glen). At 6¼ miles a signpost points R to a public footpath to Kinlochhourn. Your way continues straight ahead, becoming an increasingly poor track which wanders in attractive country, past green-humped Tor Beag (Little Hill) on the R. At Suardalan, a small farm building surrounded by a lengthy stone wall (7½ miles), you walk down between the wall and a small burn for ¼ mile, then cross the burn and strike across the heather another ¼ mile to a bridge over the Glenmore River at the edge of a forest. Go through the gate into the forest and turn R on a forest road along the forest edge. When the road ends go L along the fence (going is slow here) for several hundred yards to a gate leading R across the Allt Grannda to a shieling marked Bealachasan (8½ miles). Go S and SE for ½ mile or so across open moorland on a faint track well up on the slope above the Glenmore River until you reach the Allt a'Ghleannain (the first substantial burn). Go up the N bank (no track) until you come to a gorge too narrow to walk in, then go L across the slope for about 150yd until you meet a path going E steeply uphill parallel to the burn. Once this path is found, the way is quite visible and well cairned up and over the pass. The climb from the moorland is steep at first, slackening when you come to the ravine where a waterfall is seen ahead. The high point of land is reached just beyond the waterfall (10½ miles) and you will soon pass the Loch Coire nan Crogachan. At the top, look back − if you are lucky you will see the Cuillins of Skye and the Sound of Sleat. Beyond the loch the track drops steeply E at first, passing a path going S up the Allt Undalain valley, about halfway to the valley floor. On reaching the Allt Undalain, the track swings N and continues gently down the glen to the road at Shiel Bridge.

Glenelg

WESTER ROSS WALK
N.W. Highlands 65½ miles (105½km)

SECTION	DISTANCE		OVERNIGHT POINTS
1	16m	(26km)	Dornie-Strathcarron
2	12m	(19km)	Strathcarron-Torridon
2a	12m	(19km)	Achnashellach-Torridon
3	14½m	(23½km)	Torridon-Kinlochewe
4	11m	(18km)	Kinlochewe-Achnashellach

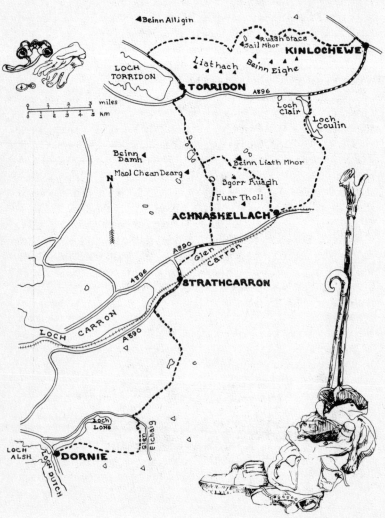

ACCOMMODATION (W.Ross)
Dornie: Dornie Hotel, several B&Bs
Strathcarron: Strathcarron Hotel at rly station, several
                 B&Bs at Coulags
Torridon: Torridon Hotel, a few B&Bs in Alligin
Kinlochewe: Kinlochewe Hotel, several B&Bs
Achnashellach: no accommodation, nearest via rly is
                 Achnasheen (2 hotels) or Strathcarron

PUBLIC TRANSPORT (H&I)
Dornie: bus Glasgow, Inverness or Kyle of Lochalsh
Strathcarron
Achnashellach } train Inverness or Kyle of Lochalsh
Torridon: minibus Strathcarron Station or postbus
   Achnasheen
Kinlochewe: postbus Achnasheen Station (1 r/t daily
   Mon-Sat); bus Inverness via Achnasheen (Tues, Thurs, Fri)

This Walk is a challenging route of great variety: from Loch Duich north via narrow valleys and rolling moorlands to Loch Carron and its wide strath; from Loch Carron over high mountain passes into Loch Torridon, one of the most spectacular sea lochs in Scotland; from Torridon by partly trackless wilderness between great mountain massifs to Kinlochewe; and on to Achnashellach through the forests and moors of the beautiful Coulin Pass. The section from Torridon to Kinlochewe has a trackless rough stretch. It should be attempted only by walkers with some previous experience in trackless areas and those who are not intimidated by wildness of scenery. The section from Dornie to Strathcarron can be shortened to 13½ miles by ending the walk at Attadale. Here the train can be used to carry you to Strathcarron (1 hotel), or to Kyle of Lochalsh (a variety of accommodation) or Achnasheen (2 hotels). From the latter two points, you can return by train the next morning to Strathcarron or Achnashellach to walk to Torridon. This shortens the distance, saves walking on the road and gives more flexibility in accommodation and the choice of the next day's journey. A circular walk can be made from Achnashellach by using sections 2a, 3 and 4.

Torridon is the centrepiece of this Walk, a mecca for hikers and climbers from all over Britain. We were first attracted to it by glowing accounts of its scenery and the hill walks, and it remains a favourite on both counts. It was there that we met a most remarkable dog, Bucko. Now gone to his reward, he was 13 and slightly deaf then, but our journal reported that he conducted us over Beinn Alligin.

121

He is a courteous bundle of fur, about the size of a fox terrier, and he patiently led the way, waiting or returning for us, if we were slow to come up. In only one place, on the Horns, did he take another route than the marked trail. His owners tell the story that he accompanied an older gentleman up Alligin one day. The mists came down and the gentleman wandered off the trail. Bucko barked furiously until the man followed him safely back to the trail and down. The gentleman swears Bucko saved his life. I can believe it. He's an odd dog, often climbs Alligin by himself. He saw us safely down to the footpath by Nobuil and then bolted home for supper. [And again the next day] Bucko has come with us again, a little footsore perhaps from yesterday's guiding. I'm convinced he isn't a dog at all – maybe a hairy prince in disguise. Of course he has a rather doggy configuration. But he is so careful on the trail, looking back constantly to see if we are coming. If I get too far ahead he goes back for Kay. Only if we stop too long at one place (unless we're eating), will he bark and then only a few apologetic yaps just to remind us that the trail (and his dinner) is ahead. When we stop and eat he never begs and accepts carefully anything offered him. He rode back on the Postbus with us, sitting on the seat and watching the scenery until the road got too twisty and then he hid on the floor (I almost joined him, the road is fairly hair-raising).

OVERNIGHT POINTS – Dornie is a small village on the shores of Loch Duich just where it meets Loch Long. It is noted for the restored Eilean Donnan, a castle much photographed because of its dramatic site on a rocky island. Its silhouette thrusts out into Loch Duich with the loch and the surrounding hills catching spectacular cloud and light effects in all seasons (castle open to the public, with tearoom and shop). Loch Duich is a gulf impressively enclosed by high hills. If you start at Dornie and want a small leg-up for the next day, there are B&Bs at Bundalloch, 1½ miles on your way. This is a quiet clachan (cluster of houses) on the shore of Loch Long, with a view of the hills across the loch and to the east. **Strathcarron** is a scattered community on the fertile land at the head of Loch Carron. **Torridon** is both the magnificent Loch Torridon, with its upper and lower lochs, and a tiny village at its head. Torridon is one of Scotland's climbing centres, the principal challenges being Liathach, the monarch, with its 3 miles of steep red sandstone terraces, Beinn Alligin, with its interesting 'Horns of Alligin' and Beinn Damh. All can be climbed by the average hiker, but Liathach can be a dangerous ridge from which to retreat in sudden bad weather and should not be attempted by inexperienced scramblers. **Kinlochewe** is a pleasant village in the heart of the mountains. Nearby is Britain's first National Nature Reserve, Beinn Eighe, containing a range of seven peaks and the woodlands of Coille na Glas-Leitire, with its stands of Scots pine. The true Scots pine has short needles and the shape of the mature tree is distinctive – its silhouette is more like a hardwood than the accepted idea of what a pine should be. Its needles are bottle green in colour while the boughs are reddish. We always believed that the destruction of the ancient forest, the Caledonian Wood, took place in the distant past so it came as a surprise to learn that many priceless remnants here at Kinlochewe (as well as at Rothiemurchus and in Strathspey) were felled during the last two world wars, to provide ammunition boxes. The islands of Loch Maree and the loch's north-facing slope have stands of these native pine, while the south-facing slope has stands of oakwood. The oakwood was used to make charcoal for smelting bog iron at Kinlochewe in the seventeenth century which in turn was used to make cannon and other items. True Caledonian forests still remain in 35 locations in Scotland. We owe the Nature Conservancy a vote of thanks, for it is largely through their efforts that some of these, like Beinn Eighe, have become the responsibility of the National Trust. The majority of the forests are held by private landowners who are encouraged to conserve by grants from local authorities. At Kinlochewe there is also an experiment in natural regeneration, so that our children may see a small return of these woods. **Achnashellach** is a lonely railway station and a small cluster of houses in Glen Carron. Mountain masses line both sides of the glen here, most notably Fuar Tholl and Sgurr Ruadh to the northwest and Moruisg to the east. The bottom and lower slopes of the glen are forested and contain great swaths of rhododendron, a handsome sight when in bloom.

cormorant

1 DORNIE–STRATHCARRON
16 miles (26km) 750 + 990ft (230 + 300m) OS 25 & 33

This is a long walk, from Loch Duich to Loch Carron by glens and moorland, past tiny clachans (villages), through sheep farms, by tumbling rivers, but mostly on deserted uplands. The way can be shortened to 13½ miles by taking the train between Strathcarron and Attadale. The footing is fair to excellent and the way is mostly easy to follow.

NORTH – Take the narrow road from Dornie to Bundalloch (1½ miles). Here the road deteriorates into a muddy cowpath at the River Glennan. The path follows the S side of the river at first, but when the river, becoming a burn, enters a ravine, the path becomes many tracks. The wetness and the many sheep and deer tracks make one continuous path impossible. However, it is easy enough to make your way up this valley by staying close to the burn. As the valley narrows, the sides get steeper and the burn smaller and you will be crossing at will. There are beautiful views of the mountains ahead, but they begin to be hidden as you work your way up the ravine. As the burn branches, always follow the deepest cut. You will eventually come to the source of the burn, a wet mossy spot. Continue up the ravine. You will pass and ignore a cairn and a path going S up and over the ridge. The OS map shows another trail soon after this which could be taken, going over the N ridge – we never found it. The safest way is to continue E up to the head of the ravine and on to the ridge of land. There, spread below you, is Glen Eichaig, with the scattered buildings of Camus-Luinie Farm at your feet. Go straight down to the farm and the road and go NW on the road towards the head of Loch Long. About 1½ miles from Camus-Luinie you will cross the River Eichaig by a long bridge. Go on past a school and over a smaller bridge, until at 7 miles the private road to Nonach Lodge goes R. Walk up past the Lodge, through some farm buildings and a field, and out on to the open moorland. Tracks along the W side of the River Ling are soon picked up (take the one nearest the river). Numerous attractive cascades and waterfalls occur for the next mile. The track keeps near the river until it crosses a burn on an old wooden bridge (8½ miles) and reaches the ruins of a shieling ¼ mile beyond. Here the track becomes more pronounced and swings uphill away from the river, keeping NE and then N until the ridge of land is reached near Carn Allt na Bradh. Loch an Iasaich can no longer be seen to the L because of new afforestation but a tiny unnamed lochan may be seen to the R. You will encounter electricity pylons near the shieling and they will keep you company all

the way into Glen Attadale. The track down into the glen passes
through a short stretch of forest and then joins an LRT in the open,
which takes you down to the floor of Glen Attadale and along the N
edge of the glen to Attadale House. On the way down there are views
of Loch Carron and the hills beyond. As the track nears the House it
enters a forest of large trees and flowering shrubs, strikingly beautiful
in the spring. It skirts the N and W sides of the House and emerges at
a door in a wall to the A890 just opposite the Attadale rly station
(13½ miles). Strathcarron station and hotel are 2½ miles N on the
A890.

SOUTH – Walk S on the A890, or take the train, to Attadale rly
station. Across the road from the station is a door in a high wall. Enter
and walk a short distance to the W side of Attadale House, pass
around the N end and take the unpaved road E along the N side of the
glen. Beyond a bridge the way becomes an LRT and climbs steadily.
Take the second gate in the deer fence, where the LRT veers L (you
will have just passed under electricity pylons), and follow an old track
through the forest to another gate leading past a reed-filled lochan on
the L out on to moorland. The track now goes S downhill to Glen
Ling and follows the W bank of the River Ling to Nonach Lodge and
the motor road. Go L (E) around the head of Loch Long, over a bridge
past a school and over the River Eichaig. In about 2 miles Camus-
Luinie will be reached. Here there is a collection of buildings, one of
which is still thatched. Go W steeply uphill from the village to the
ridge and down into the narrow ravine of the Glennan River,
following it to Bundalloch on Loch Long. Dornie is 1½ miles to the L
on a narrow road.

Camus-Luinie

2 STRATHCARRON–TORRIDON
12 miles (19km) 1310ft (400m) OS 24 & 25

Loch Torridon

This walk is similar to the one from Achnashellach to Torridon, but over less high ground. It shares the same path at the Torridon end. Starting from Strathcarron station, it crosses the wide valley of the River Carron; goes up the long, narrow valley of the Fionn-abhainn burn to the Bealach na Lice (400m) and then down to spectacular Loch Torridon. We did this walk on a misty day and it was our first experience in finding our way under such circumstances. Being basically cowards, we own to a shade of anxiety as we puzzled our way through the mist, with map and compass in very close attendance. We knew our anxiety was unreasonable, for the path remained well in evidence a few yards ahead and behind us; the landmarks turned up regularly; and the weather remained mild if murky. Once over the pass the mist and our courage rose simultaneously and, brave as lions, we swung down to our night's lodging. The moral of the tale is – obey your common sense and not your fears.

NORTH – Leave Strathcarron station NW on the A890. You have a choice of: (a) staying on the A890 to the bridge over the Fionn-abhainn or (b) leaving the A890 in about ½ mile where a lane goes R to New Kelso Farm. Go past the farm to a path by the River Carron and along the river bank to the edge of a plantation where a track goes N to rejoin the A890 (2 miles). At the bridge over the Fionn-abhainn go up a path along the E side of the burn. Three handsome waterfalls are passed in a ½ mile stretch. About 1½ miles from the A890 you will cross the burn on a wooden bridge; go up the W side of the burn, past a shieling, to Loch Coire Fionnaraich. The loch is distinctive for

126

sea thrift

its red sand beaches, composed of Torridon sandstone which crops out from Strathcarron north to Sutherland and is most prominent around Torridon. From the loch, the path climbs over the Bealach na Lice (400m), joining the path from Achnashellach ¼ mile before the bealach. ½ mile before the loch, an alternative higher path goes L steeply uphill to 580m and around the S shoulder of Maol Chean-dearg, rejoining the path over the Bealach na Lice at Loch an Eion, ½ mile beyond the pass. From Loch an Eion, the way winds over a flat, rocky and loch-studded plateau, then goes down to Annat and the A896. The Alligin–Diabaig road is 1¼ miles to the R.

SOUTH – Follow the description for the Achnashellach–Torridon section to Loch an Eion. Here there are two alternatives: (a) around the N end of the loch, over the Bealach na Lice and E and SE down to the Loch Coire Fionnaraich and the Fionn-abhainn burn to the A890 at Coulags; or (b) around the W side of Loch an Eion and the S shoulder of Maol Chean-dearg to the (a) path. From Coulags go SW, then SE on the A890 to Strathcarron station; or in ½ mile take a track S beside a plantation to a path which follows the River Carron to New Kelso, the A890 and the station.

2a ACHNASHELLACH–TORRIDON
12 miles (19km) 2120ft (645m) OS 24 & 25

A lovely high rock and heather walk from wooded Glen Carron through mountain fastnesses to Loch Torridon, a magnificent sea loch bordered by the red sandstone peaks of Beinn Alligin, Liathach and Beinn Damh. The path climbs steeply out of Achnashellach station to the imposing and desolate Coire Lair, then winds through ever-changing mountain scenery by three high bealachs (mountain passes), one at 645m. It goes by half a dozen lochs and lochans, before coming down to the head of Loch Torridon.

We have done the walk in mist and in sun. While, of course, a clear day is preferred (the views are superb) a misty day makes the walk more mysterious, with tantalising glimpses of high peaks as the clouds lift momentarily. In both conditions, there is a strong feeling of being in the midst of the mountains, with mankind very far away. However, the way is easy to find in clear *or* cloudy weather and there is little danger of straying from the path.

NORTH – Walk SW on the rly line past the stationmaster's house (note his beautiful flower garden) and turn up a well-worn path alongside a deer fence, where a large white sign is marked 'Coire Lair' very faintly. (From the A890, the way to the station is not marked. It is about ¼ mile S of the hamlet of Achnashellach. A private road (so marked) by a telephone kiosk leads in a short distance to the station.) From the station an alternative route is to take the forestry road crossing the rly line just S of the station, turning L at the first crossroads, going to the end of the road, and taking a boggy but clear track through the woods to the main path. The forest is left behind as the path zig-zags steeply up to the Coire Lair (the Coire of the Mare). Just beyond two rude stone shelters, the path forks twice. Take the R fork and then the L fork, going past the N side of Loch Coire Lair to the head of the coire and over a pass at 645m between Beinn Liath Mhor (the Great Grey Mountain) and Sgorr Ruadh (the Rocky Red Peak). Beyond, the path descends around the shoulder of Sgorr Ruadh to Bealach Ban (the Fair Pass) (550m), then slants down to join the path coming up the Fionn-abhainn (the White River) from Strathcarron. Turn R uphill over Bealach na Lice (400m) and down around the N end of Loch an Eion. Here, another path enters from the L and the way leads NW across the flats between Lochan Domhain and Loch an Uillt-bheithe down to Annat on the A896, 1¼ miles from the intersection of the A896 and the Alligin–Diabaig road. Loch Torridon Hotel is ¾ mile to the L.

SOUTH – Walk SW from Annat on the A896 and the track will be seen leading E uphill. It forks shortly. Take the R fork. The path is well trodden and well cairned at difficult spots. At Loch an Eion, go N around the loch and over the pass of Bealach na Lice. Watch for a path leading L along the slope, carrying you over Bealach Ban into Coire Lair, mostly in an E direction. At the lower end of the coire, the path from Coulin enters from the L and a second path shortly comes in from the R. Your way then is SE and S, the path dropping down the Lair valley to Glen Carron and the rly station at Achnashellach.

cow parsley

3 TORRIDON–KINLOCHEWE
14½ miles (23¼km) 1475ft (450m) OS 19, 24 & 25

Liathach

This walk is a strenuous one through wild country, with high mountains on every hand. You will journey from a tiny village on a sea loch, Torridon, to another village near the head of an inland loch, Maree. Both these lochs usually make the Scottish calendars each year, but the handsome country through which you will pass does not, being hidden from the easy view of motorists. With clear weather the way is easy to find, even though 3 miles of it are trackless. However, we recommend it only for the experienced walker, because in rain, wind or low visibility the path-finding is more difficult and the walk quite a tiring one. In bad weather or for less experienced walkers we suggest walking the 'Round of Liathach' and using the Postbus as an alternative (see below).

EAST – From Torridon village go W on the motor road along the N shore of Loch Torridon. At 2½ miles there is a car park and a signposted path, the Coire Mhic Nobuil, which goes NE and E round the N side of Liathach. At about 4½ miles, shortly after passing Lochan a'Choire Dhuibh, another path leads off to the L. Go N on this new path around the flanks of Sail Mhor. At 6 miles from the car park, this path swings SE and climbs into the high Coire Mhic Fhearchair (worth the climb). However, here you leave the path and go E across country for 3 miles, following the 400m contour along the N slopes of Ruadh-stac Mhor and Ruadh-stac Beag until you pick up a path running E down to the A832. Kinlochewe is ½ mile to the R.

WEST – Go N for ½ mile on the A832 from Kinlochewe to a sign-posted path L into the Beinn Eighe Nature Reserve. Follow this path W for about 3 miles, climbing steadily to a height of 450m, and then descending slightly to the Allt Toll a'Ghiubhais where the path peters out. Go W from here, keeping along the 400m contour, first on the N slope of Ruadh-stac Beag, then across a valley and finally on the N slope of Ruadh-stac Mhor. Continue on the 400m contour, swinging SW around Ruadh-stac Mhor, crossing below Coire Mhic Fhearchair, and striking a path coming down from the coire, at 6 miles. This path goes S to join, at 7½ miles, the Coire Mhic Nobuil path going around the N side of Liathach. Go W and then SW on this path to the motor road which runs along the N shore of Loch Torridon (12 miles). Inveralligin is 2 miles to the W and Torridon village is 2½ miles to the E.

ALTERNATIVE – The Round of Liathach

EAST – Use the above route to Lochan a'Choire Dhuibh but continue E past the turnoff down the Coire Dubh Mor to the A896. The distance is 8 miles from the car park at the beginning of the Coire Mhic Nobuil path to the A896. Kinlochewe is 6¼ miles E on the A896 and Torridon village is 3¾ miles W. We recommend using the Postbus between Kinlochewe and the Coire Dubh Mor path.

WEST – The Coire Dubh Mor path is signposted on the A896. Coming from Kinlochewe, it is 3¼ miles from the Coulin Estate signpost. The Postbus driver will know the location of the path.

Alligin

4 KINLOCHEWE–ACHNASHELLACH
11 miles (18km) 810ft (274m) OS 25

Beinn Eighe

This is one of the most beautiful tracks in Scotland. It is well marked and has excellent footing. Although it is designated a footpath, it is an LRT all the way. There are several locked gates and few marks of vehicles; so our experience of walking in complete solitude is probably typical. The Achnashellach Forest is made up of a variety of conifers, including many of giant size – a rare sight in Scotland! There are three highlights to the walk. One is an intimate view from a wooden bridge where you will see the water plunging straight down through a green mossy world of shiny holly leaves, lace-like ferns and delicate woodland flowers. Another is the transition from the dense old forest with its variety of specimens to the newly planted one where the uniform trees all stand at attention in neat rows like soldiers. Finally, there is the constant view north of the long vista of Glen Coulin, ending in the stunning mass of Beinn Eighe. The south-to-north way has this view and Achnashellach is an easier starting than ending point, considering the problems of accommodation and train connections, but either way is a gorgeous ramble.

SOUTH – Leave Kinlochewe on the A896 going towards Torridon. The private road to Coulin Lodge goes off to the L at 3 miles. Follow this road along the E shore of Loch Clair. At a bridge leading to the Lodge, a sign directs you to the footpath. This footpath is a very good LRT all the way to Achnashellach. At the next bridge you will have two choices: either keeping on the NE side of Loch Coulin and climbing on a rather barren hillside above the loch, or crossing the bridge to the R and walking along the SW loch shore through pleasant forest planting. The two ways join at the head of the loch. From there continue along the River Coulin until it is crossed on a stone bridge where the way forks. The R fork goes uphill to join the Achnashellach–Torridon path. The main track continues ahead, climbing into the Coulin Pass and down through an old forest to the rly station at Achnashellach.

NORTH – Starting at Achnashellach station, cross the tracks on a forest road just to the S of the platform; go through a gate and uphill to a crossroads. Continue straight ahead, passing a sign prohibiting vehicles. The stony road climbs gradually through a magnificent old forest. The road levels off as it parallels Glen Carron. It soon climbs steadily to the Coulin Pass, where the old forest gives way to a new and uniform forest, which in turn gives way to open moorland beyond the last gate. With good visibility you will have a clear view of the Coulin Glen with Beinn Eighe dominating the skyline. The way is level or gradually descending from here to the A896. Cross the stone bridge over the River Coulin and walk N along the W side of the river into a group of farm buildings, noted Coulin on the map. Keep following the LRT which goes along the SW shore of the loch until you come to a wooden footbridge. Cross it to avoid intruding on the privacy of the Lodge and go out the main estate road to the A896, where Kinlochewe lies 3 miles to the R.

LOCH BROOM WALK
N.W. Highlands 27 miles (43½km)

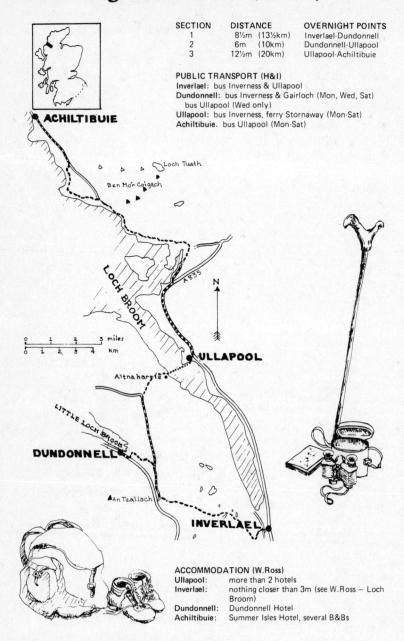

SECTION	DISTANCE		OVERNIGHT POINTS
1	8½m	(13½km)	Inverlael-Dundonnell
2	6m	(10km)	Dundonnell-Ullapool
3	12½m	(20km)	Ullapool-Achiltibuie

PUBLIC TRANSPORT (H&I)

Inverlael: bus Inverness & Ullapool
Dundonnell: bus Inverness & Gairloch (Mon, Wed, Sat)
   bus Ullapool (Wed only)
Ullapool: bus Inverness, ferry Stornaway (Mon-Sat)
Achiltibuie. bus Ullapool (Mon-Sat)

ACHILTIBUIE

Loch Tuath

Ben Mór Coigach

LOCH BROOM

A 835

N

0   1   2   3 miles
0   1   2   3   4 km

ULLAPOOL

Altnaharra?

LITTLE LOCH BROOM

DUNDONNELL

An Teallach

INVERLAEL

ACCOMMODATION (W.Ross)

Ullapool:	more than 2 hotels
Inverlael:	nothing closer than 3m (see W.Ross — Loch Broom)
Dundonnell:	Dundonnell Hotel
Achiltibuie:	Summer Isles Hotel, several B&Bs

A sea-loched route that wanders by old tracks and paths along or near the rock-girt coast of northern Wester Ross, by heather ridges, wooded glens and a coastal path. It moves from the head of Loch Broom to Achiltibuie opposite the Summer Isles. It includes a pleasant ride in a small open passenger ferry across Loch Broom, the amenities of Ullapool, the most northerly of the towns on the west coast, and the scenic 'Rock Path' near Achiltibuie. Going north the country grows progressively more deserted, the scenery more wild, with widening sweeps of sea, sky and land. The route is easy to follow, the footing fair to excellent, the sections short. Two great mountains are passed. An Teallach (The Forge, 1060m), a firm favourite of climbers, is a distinctive massif of ten peaks on the south side of Little Loch Broom. Ben Mor Coigach (740m) borders the north shore of Loch Broom, rising steeply from the water and leaving little room for the path you take.

OVERNIGHT POINTS – Inverlael is a scattered farming settlement in the fertile valley of Strath Mor at the head of Loch Broom, contained by steep hills. 4 miles south, just off the A835, is Corrieshalloch Gorge, a deep and narrow chasm containing the fine Falls of Measach. The chasm has a footbridge over it for viewing. **Dundonnell** lies in Strath Beag at the head of Little Loch Broom, another scattered farming settlement. It is overlooked by the great red Torridon sandstone peaks of An Teallach. 3 miles southeast at Corrie Hallie there is a footpath along the Allt Gleann Chaorachain which visits three waterfalls in 1½ miles. The eighteenth-century Dundonnell House has Chinese and Japanese gardens. **Ullapool** is a small fishing town, established in 1788 to further the herring industry. It is now also a resort town. The Loch Broom Highland Museum in the town centre highlights early life in the area. Motor launches run regular tours around Loch Broom and to the Summer Isles, in the summer season. **Achiltibuie** is a remote fishing village on Baden Bay, in which lie the Summer Isles. The village stretches out along several miles of a narrow road which runs parallel to a wide sandy and rocky beach. The mass of Ben Mor Coigach looms to the southeast and other isolated peaks can be seen to the north.

1 INVERLAEL-DUNDONNELL
8½ miles (13½km) 1345ft (410m) OS 19 & 20

This walk is a leg-stretching one on an old track from the head of Loch Broom to Dundonnell on Little Loch Broom. It goes over the high ridge between the two lochs with the peak of An Teallach prominently displayed. It is mostly in the open, having excellent views of the lochs and the mountains around them. The footing is fair to good and, except for a few places, the track is well in evidence.

WEST – Leave the A835 about ½ mile S of the head of Loch Broom (6 miles from Braemore Junction where the A832 goes over to Dundonnell) at a road signposted 'Letters', 'Logie'. Go W on this road a short distance past an intersection (Inverbroom Lodge to the L, Letters and Logie to the R) to Croftown, a small cluster of houses at the foot of the ridge. Go R around the end house and strike a path going L up along the edge of a plantation. At the NW corner of this forest, turn N uphill and pass a shieling on the L. The old track then zigzags and is difficult to follow in places. Watch for overgrown cuts in the hillside (where earth has been removed) as clues for finding the path. You pass through a gate and the track begins to level off. Loch Broom comes into view briefly, with a sharp drop down to it from the edge of the track. Welcome cairns will appear, to take you over the ridge. The way is up, down and around low hills, passing several lochs and over two causeways, one quite substantial. As the track begins to descend, better ground is encountered, supporting sheep and flowers. An Teallach (1060m) comes into view across Strath Beag (the valley of the Dundonnell river). The track crosses several streams, finally turning downhill just above a handsome waterfall (worth a small digression), and descending to an open deciduous forest. Here the track is overgrown and difficult to stay on but just choose what seems the best way down to the valley floor to a farm track along the Dundonnell river. Go R on this track to a gate and then L a few yards to a bridge over the river, leading to the A832. The Dundonnell Hotel is 2 miles to the R. A more pleasant way is by the farm road to the R

136

which goes on the N side of the river, through Eilean Darach, over a footbridge through a farmyard and out to the A832 and the Dundonnell Hotel.

EAST – Leave the Dundonnell Hotel and go E on the A832 about ½ mile to a farm road on the L by a telephone kiosk. Go through the farmyard to a rough farm track leading E to a wooden footbridge over the Dundonnell river. Cross to a path to Eilean Darach and go by the estate road to a narrow paved road to Dundonnell House. Continue on to the buildings just before a bridge recrosses the river to join the A832. Do not go to the A832 but continue along the river keeping L and going through a gate. Immediately after the gate, go slanting uphill SE through an open forest until a faint track is picked up. It is overgrown with small bushes until above the forest and need only be kept neat until the forest edge is reached. About ¼ mile above the forest the track climbs steeply past a waterfall and crosses the stream above it. The way is now across open grazing which gradually grows rougher, finally becoming heather. Beyond one burn (at 136852) the track is quite difficult to follow but 200yd ahead a cut in the hillside will show you where it goes. Cairns are soon picked up, to carry you over the ridge and down to the head of Loch Broom.

NOTE: If this section is being combined with the Dundonnell–Ullapool section, in going W take the road along the N side of the Dundonnell river to Eilean Darach and go R along the road signposted 'Badrallach'. Done together, the two sections are 12 miles in length. Unless you have made arrangements to spend the night at the Altnaharrie Inn you must remember the ferry schedule from Altnaharrie to Ullapool in your timing. See note at the end of section 2.

Loch Broom

2 DUNDONNELL–ULLAPOOL
6 miles (10km) 770ft (236m) OS 19

path's end

This is a short, easy walk, mostly on estate roads, from Little Loch Broom to Loch Broom. The way is through varied countryside, by farmland along a river, up through a larch forest, over heather-covered moorland with wide views of lochs and mountains, down to the inn at Altnaharrie and a ride in an open ferry across Loch Broom to Ullapool. The way is clear and the footing good to excellent. A unique feature of this walk is the setting of the inn at Altnaharrie. There are not many civilised spots today that can be reached only by boat or foot. The view from it would be worth a trek of twice the distance.

NORTH – Leave the Dundonnell Hotel and go E on the A832 about ½ mile to a farm road on the L by a telephone kiosk. Go through the farmyard to a rough cart track leading E to a wooden footbridge over the Dundonnell river. Cross to a path to Eilean Darach and go by the estate road to a narrow paved road coming from Dundonnell House (this is the same route as the first part of the **EAST** walk in section 1). Here your way is L, signposted 'Badrallach'. The road climbs steadily but gradually up through a larch forest. When it leaves the forest there are views of the hills to the S, with the higher peaks of An Teallach perhaps having snow on them (as late as mid-May). As you continue, you get a view of the head of Little Loch Broom, with the Dundonnell Hotel standing alone, white against the hillside. The little hill of Creag na Ceapaich soon cuts off this view but as you approach the junction where the track to Altnaharrie leaves the road, another view of Little

Loch Broom with a single house on the shore can be seen. The turnoff for Altnaharrie (Burn of the Boundary) is easily identified as it is just where the paved road takes a sharp turn to the L and begins to descend. The cart track goes off R, through a gate and across a saddle, with Loch Broom coming into view. The track skirts the small Loch na h-Airbhe (Boundary Loch) on your R, becoming rough and descending steeply to the buildings of Altnaharrie Inn on the shore of Loch Broom. There is a ferry to Ullapool operated by the Inn.

SOUTH – From Ullapool take the ferry to Altnaharrie, which leaves from the pier. The track from Altnaharrie goes steeply uphill on moorland from behind the hotel, with excellent views back to Loch Broom and Ullapool. As the slope lessens, Loch na h-Airbhe is passed and at 1 mile the narrow paved road to Dundonnell (to the L) is reached. The road passes under the cliffs of Beinn nam Ban and descends gradually through a larch forest into Strath Beag. Where the road turns L at the river, go R on the estate road of Eilean Darach, to a footpath and footbridge over the river to a farm track leading to the A832 ½ mile from the Dundonnell Hotel.

NOTE: Infrequently in bad weather the ferry between Altnaharrie and Ullapool may not run. Call the Altnaharrie Inn (tel. 085 483 230) if in doubt. The Inn (or the Information Centre at Ullapool) will tell you the schedule. If you are going N and are at Dundonnell and the ferry is not running, in order to honour your reservation in Ullapool, you will have to retrace the Inverlael–Dundonnell walk in time to catch the Inverness–Ullapool bus *unless* it is M, W, or Sat, in which case there is a morning bus to Ullapool from Dundonnell.

silverweed

3 ULLAPOOL–ACHILTIBUIE
12½ miles (20km) 750ft (230m) OS 15 & 19

Achiltibuie beach

This is a beautiful coastal walk, much of it on the ancient footpath linking the remote fishing village of Achiltibuie with Ullapool. It includes the 'Rock Path' which hugs the coast just under the cliffs of Ben Mor Coigach. There are constant views out to sea, with the fabled Summer Isles appearing near Achiltibuie. Seabirds are abundant company for the walk. The path is easily followed but certainly earns its name of the 'Rock Path'. The going should not be hurried in this section so allow ample time. The 5-mile section just north of Ullapool is all on the motor road and it can be avoided, if desired, by taking a taxi from Ullapool. Because the 'Rock Path' is close to, but high above, the sea edge in places, it should not be attempted in poor visibility. Achiltibuie, that small village near the end of a long, winding narrow road from Ullapool, stands out in our Scottish reflections as a rare jewel. Here, many Julys ago, we spent an unbelievably warm two weeks of unbroken sunshine, living in a converted mill which a Scottish family loaned us. This offer (they were complete strangers, albeit friends of friends) was one of those generous gestures of friendliness to visitors we so often experience in Scotland. Here the wonders of the sea were introduced to our budding six-year-old scientist and two pictures remain with us: one of him in Wellingtons wading by the hour in the tidal pools, head bent, earnestly observing that natural laboratory; the other of him triumphantly struggling home with a large salmon in his arms. This purchase was carefully opened and its inner workings examined minutely before the subsequent feast. Happy memories of an enchanted spot!

140

NORTH – Leave Ullapool and go N on the A835. In about 3½ miles the road reaches and skirts Loch Kanaird. At 5 miles there is a signpost to Keanchulish House and here the estate road is taken. Go N about 1 mile to a bridge across the River Kanaird. Cross and turn W through a wicket gate in a deer fence from which the path climbs steeply to 230m. If you have the time and energy, just after the bridge go SW to the bay of Camas Mor and visit Dun Canna, a ruined broch on a rocky promontory. Back on the path, beyond the top of the rise, you will encounter cairns and posts and it is vital to keep them in view in order to stay on the path. In the next 4 miles you are on the 'Rock Path', with high hills at first on your R and then the cliffs of Ben Mor Coigach, 743m. At Geodha Mor, where the Garbh Allt is crossed, there is a small beach which is a pleasant spot for lunch. Beyond it the path passes under the cliffs of the Ben and comes out at Culnacraig to a narrow motor road. Here there are two choices: by path along the coast to Achduart and a road to the Youth Hostel at Acheninver and on to Achiltibuie, or by the road to Achiltibuie. The hotel and B&Bs are all on the motor road some 3–4 miles N of Culnacraig.

SOUTH – Walk SE on the motor road to Culnacraig and pick up the coastal path just beyond the houses. Watch for posts marking the path, as the heather hides it in places. About 4 miles beyond Culnacraig the path descends steeply and the River Kanaird and a bridge can be seen ahead. Cross the bridge and turn S along the river and sea loch on an estate road to the A835. Ullapool is 5 miles to the R.

ASSYNT WALK N.W. Highlands
41 miles (66km)

SECTION	DISTANCE		OVERNIGHT POINTS
1	13m	(21km)	Elphin-Lochinver
2	15m	(24km)	Lochinver-Inchnadamph
3	13m	(21km)	Inchnadamph-Drumbeg

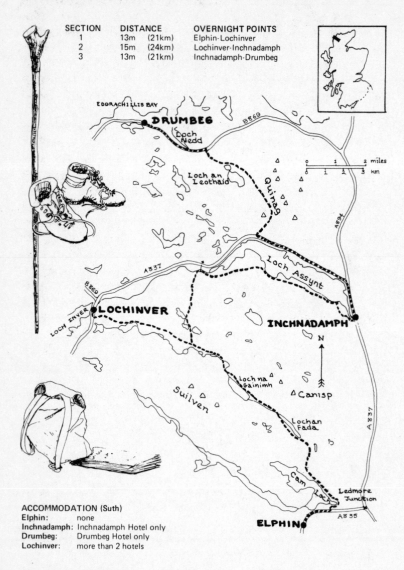

ACCOMMODATION (Suth)
Elphin: none
Inchnadamph: Inchnadamph Hotel only
Drumbeg: Drumbeg Hotel only
Lochinver: more than 2 hotels

PUBLIC TRANSPORT (H&I)
bus from all overnight points to Lairg; train Lairg to Inverness (Mon-Sat)

142

This is the most northerly of our routes and takes us through the austere landscape of Sutherland, the southern province of the Viking Earls of Orkney. Of all Scotland, Sutherland gives the feeling of being the most remote from the hand of man. It has a stark beauty, with vast sweeps of heather, dotted with lochs, and with isolated mountain massifs thrusting up from low hills. Even on a bright day the land seems inhospitable, and on a grey and lowering day can look positively ominous. Yet the MacLeods of Assynt and other Sutherland clans wrested a living from the granite and heather, as the ruins of their shielings attest. For those with a modicum of courage and a taste for real solitude, the walk from Elphin, by the coastal fishing village of Lochinver and the sport-fishing centre of Inchnadamph to remote Drumbeg, cannot be equalled. The great peaks of Suilven, Canisp and Quinag will often be in view. Red deer will be seen on the hillsides and grouse will startle you as they whirr into the air ahead of you or entertain you as they 'grouse' in the heather (you will know by their grumbling complaining cry how the term 'to grouse' came into our language). An occasional duck will squatter away into flight from the lochs as you pass. But mostly there is only the wind to keep you company as you stride along.

OVERNIGHT POINTS – **Elphin** is a tiny hamlet in a lonely setting of mountains and lochs on the Ross–Sutherland border on the fringes of the wild Assynt country. **Lochinver** is an attractive small resort on a sea loch. The surrounding area is a maze of tiny lochans and is well known for its fishing. **Inchnadamph**, at the eastern end of Loch Assynt, is little more than the comfortable Inchnadamph Hotel. Nearby are the ruins of Ardvreck Castle, and seventeenth-century Calda House, once the home of the MacKenzies. Ardvreck Castle was built c.1490 by the MacLeods, and it was here, in 1650, that the great Marquis of Montrose was betrayed by the local laird. Just to the south, the Allt nam Uamh bone caves show traces of occupation by early man. Ben More Assynt (995m) 4 miles to the southeast, is the highest mountain in the county. There is good fishing and a wealth of day's walks in the area. **Drumbeg** lies on a narrow and steep coastal road, facing Eddrachillis Bay. It is a tiny little village, noted for its fishing. There are magnificent views in all directions. A little craft shop attractively housed in an old building has one of the finest choices of Scottish-made items we have come across.

1 ELPHIN–LOCHINVER
13 miles (21km) 400ft (120m) OS 15

Suilven from E

This walk is strenuous but rewarding, over typical Sutherland land-scape, all granite, lochs and heather. The way lies between Suilven (731m) and Canisp (846m). The extraordinary experience of Suilven is the reward of this walk. The view of it from the coastal village of Lochinver is so completely different from that at Elphin, it is only possible to comprehend it as the same mountain by walking round it. Starting from Elphin it shows as a sharp obelisk reminiscent of the Matterhorn. As you come abreast of it, it stretches out as a long pinnacled mass, with the sharp eastern peak just a thumb on the serrated ridge that is now dominated at its western end by a fortress-like dome. Coming down into Lochinver it is startling to look back and see that the view is now comprised solely of this dome, looking like a giant haystack. A small challenge in path-finding is found at the Elphin end between Cam Loch and Lochan Fada, but from Lochan Fada to Lochinver the way is clearly visible. Footing is fair to excellent. The recommended direction is Elphin to Lochinver since Elphin affords no accommodation. Also the footing grows easier in this direction as the walk progresses.

NORTHWEST – Halfway between Elphin and Ledmore Junction on the A835 just E of the bridge over the Na Luirgean burn, a faint track wanders NW from a gravel pit, towards the E end of Cam Loch. It is easier to cut due N from the gravel pit to the end of the loch and pick up the track by the shore. The track goes along the NE shore of the loch, leaving it in about 2 miles, going uphill along the same heading. When the loch again comes into view ahead, turn R and go N along a rising broad rocky ridge (there is a nearly-buried ruin of an old stone wall to follow at first). You will soon see cairns and they will carry you all the way to the NW end of Lochan Fada, with the track to Lochinver becoming increasingly visible. The track crosses the Allt a Ghlinne Dorcha just to the W end of Lochan Fada, on makeshift stepping stones (it may be a bit wet crossing after heavy rain but hardly dangerous). From Lochan Fada the track is well defined and in good condition all the way to Canisp Lodge, where a paved road goes down to the S end of Lochinver. There are several branching tracks but the main track to Lochinver going steadily NW is not easily mistaken. Lochan na Gainimh has a flank of Suilven plunging steeply into it, making an impressive picture. At Suileag there is a shieling (still roofed in 1979), surrounded by a Cyclopean wall, well worth a short digression. At Canisp Lodge, keep to the R of the main building, joining the paved road just beyond.

Suilven from N

SOUTHEAST – From the PO go S on the A837 to the paved road on the L, about 100yd before the road turns out to the pier. (This road, not shown as leading to Canisp Lodge in 1979, was merely marked 'Private'.) Go E to Canisp Lodge, L around the back of the main building, through a gate to a rough track going E. The track is well in evidence. There are a number of forks that may try to lure you off the Elphin track so check your map at each one. At Lochan Fada, take the path on its S shore. Here the track begins to grow faint and cairns appear. About ½ mile beyond Lochan Fada the track swings S and Cam Loch comes into view a mile away. If it is misty and the cairns are lost, any compass heading between SE and SW (with S preferable) will bring you to the shore of Cam Loch, which can be followed L to its SE end where ¼ mile S across country will bring you to the A835.

Suilven from W

2 LOCHINVER–INCHNADAMPH
15 miles (24km) 650ft (200m) OS 15

This is a 'lang walk i' the heather', half of it along the shore of Loch Assynt, with constant views of Quinag (808m) to the north and the hills of Glencanisp Forest to the south. The track stops rather abruptly about 5 miles from the Inchnadamph end, so some of the walk is a constant challenge in finding the easiest way. One cannot get lost as the route lies along the shore of Loch Assynt. It is not possible to hug the shore itself, and deciding just how high to go as well as picking your way along this contour line is fun but tiring. For this reason you may want to shorten the walk by using the bus at the western end between Lochinver and Little Assynt. The real challenge is deciding how to negotiate the flat marshy section at Inchnadamph which includes getting across the river. The water when we were there was about knee-deep and the land on either side so wet that casting about for the best place to cross was making us as wet as plunging straight in – which we finally did, the smaller author piggyback on the larger with much staggering and laughter. Because it is less unpleasant to finish than to start out wet and, should the bus be used, it is easier to arrange your timing at the beginning, we recommend the west to east direction.

EAST – There are several ways to Little Assynt from Lochinver: (a) follow the walk to Elphin as far as Suileag (Section 1, **SOUTHEAST** 3½ miles), taking the L fork there and going N by Loch Crom and Loch an Leothaid to the bridge over Assynt Water to Little Assynt (7 miles); (b) follow the walk to Elphin as far as Canisp Lodge (1½ miles) and go N on the track to Inveruptan and the A837 (3½ miles), then by the A837 to Little Assynt (6 miles); (c) take a footpath along the S side of Assynt Water, leaving the A837 just before the bridge at the N end of Lochinver. This footpath joins a section of the old motor road in about 2 miles and the newer road (A837) at 2½ miles, reaching Little Assynt at 5 miles; or (d) take the morning bus from Lochinver PO to Little Assynt. This will shorten the walk to about 8 miles.

Just E of Little Assynt (a single house) a track goes S crossing Assynt Water to meet the track coming up from Suileag and a track going E. Take the latter, which crosses the Rubh an Alt-toir peninsula, coming out to the shore of Loch Assynt 2½ miles from Little Assynt. Go along the shore to an extensive ruined shieling (worth an exploration). The track is visible and in good condition. Beyond the ruins there is no path and we struck off across country parallel to the loch at a distance of a few yards for some ¼ mile. The way is through heather, boggy in places, or in open birch forests with fine footing on short grasses. Take the easiest line of travel, contouring (ie staying at the same elevation) whenever possible. At An Coimhleun Forest, the way near the shore is blocked by high cliffs. Just before these cliffs a wide gully goes S steeply uphill through the forest, coming out on a broad heather slope leading down to the River Loanon. A deer fence at the end of the heather must be climbed (or crawled under), an expanse of very wet ground negotiated and the river forded. Go S upstream along the river bank until you reach riffles. The water here is 12–18in deep, the bottom gravel. If the river is in spate and too deep to cross near the loch, go upstream until it grows shallow enough to cross or on to Stronechrubie, a mile or so upstream where there is a bridge. Inchnadamph Hotel is on the A837 at the mouth of the River Loanon, 1½ miles N of Stronechrubie.

WEST – Leave the entrance of the Inchnadamph Hotel and negotiate a wide bog, the River Loanon and a deer fence. A very wide heather slope goes W uphill. The N edge of the slope terminates at first in a cliff dropping to Loch Assynt but the cliff gives way to a steep gully at the first cluster of birch trees, leading down to an open forest. The way beyond is the reverse of the **EAST** directions.

Lochinver

3 INCHNADAMPH–DRUMBEG
13 miles (21km) 820ft (250m) OS 15

Ardvreck Castle

This walk is across typical Sutherland scenery. It goes from Inchnadamph with its comfortable fishing hotel, along Loch Assynt, up to the flanks of the serrated ridge of Quinag, and down Gleann Leireag to Drumbeg on the many-islanded Eddrachillis Bay. The views are superb – into Eddrachillis Bay and one of its fingers, Loch Nedd, the towering bulk of Quinag, and the long narrow Loch Assynt. While much of the walk is on motor roads (violating our rule on this), they are lightly used. The footing is good to excellent, the way easily found. We walked this on what must be a typical Sutherland day, mostly rainy but with flashes of sun. The previous afternoon we had arrived by Postbus at Drumbeg, a rather unnerving but scenic journey by a winding, steep narrow road. On foot, the road became a delight, with time to appreciate the slowly changing views of sea lochs, hills and burns. As we set out, a friendly wave from the Drumbeg postmistress (who had found us a place to stay in answer to our transatlantic letter to her) reminded us yet again of the warmth of Scottish hearts.

NORTH – Take the A837 6½ miles to Tumore (4 miles beyond the junction of the A894 and the A837). At Tumore (a single house) go over a fence to the L of the house and around a stone wall to a burn at the back. Ford the burn to a track which slants R NE up the slope of Creag na h-Iolaire (Crag of the Eagle) to a pass, the Bealach Leireag. The track swings NW and descends gently down the Gleann Leireag. Quinag (local pronunciation sounds like 'cognac') bulks to the R. By Loch an Leothaid, the track becomes faint and cairns appear. The way

148

traverses the N shore of Loch Uidh na h-larna and the Abhainn Gleann Leireag, leaving the burn to strike the B869. The Drumbeg PO and Hotel are 2¾ miles to the L.

SOUTH – Walk E from Drumbeg along the B869, a winding narrow road, passing Nedd at 1½ miles. The turnoff is at 2¾ miles from the Drumbeg Hotel, about ½ mile E of the head of Loch Nedd. A small burn parallels the road here to the R. There is a large cairn on the R just past a clump of trees, with a rectangular concrete cistern just opposite. The track leads from the cairn down along a fence for about 50yd, then swings E and is well cairned all the way to Loch Uidh na h-larna. It is easy to wander off on enticing sheep tracks here but if your way peters out in the heather, backtrack and look for the next cairn. The way is above the Abhainn Gleann Leireag burn, an easy up-and-down trail. You will be walking directly towards the bulk of Quinag until the head of Loch an Leothaid. Along this loch an unmistakable track is met, which carries you to Loch Assynt. Past Loch an Leothaid it rises gently to a U-shaped saddle and Loch Assynt comes into view, with Canisp and Suilven beyond. The track leads down a bit more steeply to a white house at Tumore and the A837. It is 6½ miles to the R to Lochinver and 6 miles to the L to Inchnadamph. On the road to Inchnadamph, about a mile beyond Skiag Bridge where the road joins the A894, there are two ruins: Ardvreck Castle, on a promontory jutting into Loch Assynt, and Calda House, just off the road on the shore. The modest hump of a chambered cairn will be noted on the short walk to the castle.

Quinag

ARRAN WALK Islands
34½ miles (56km)

SECTION	DISTANCE		OVERNIGHT POINTS
1	11m	(18km)	Lagg-Lamlash
2	4½m	(7km)	Lamlash-Brodick
3	11m	(18km)	Brodick-Corrie
4	8m	(13km)	Corrie-Lochranza

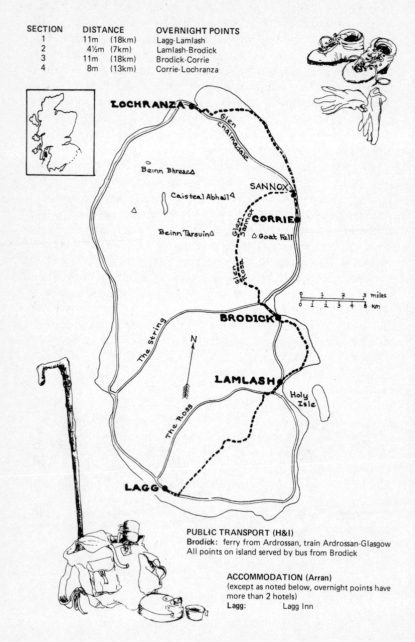

PUBLIC TRANSPORT (H&I)
Brodick: ferry from Ardrossan, train Ardrossan-Glasgow
All points on island served by bus from Brodick

ACCOMMODATION (Arran)
(except as noted below, overnight points have
more than 2 hotels)
Lagg: Lagg Inn

150

This route explores Arran, a fascinating 10-by-20-mile island in the Firth of Clyde. The island compresses into its small confines a microcosm of Scotland, from its magnificent mountainous north, capped by Goat Fell (874m), to the rolling moors and farmlands in the south. In spite of its closeness to densely populated Glasgow, Arran is sparsely settled, with the settlements only on the coast, leaving the interior a wilderness, especially in the north. The route can be combined with climbs up the Arran mountains, most of which are well within the capability of the average walker. The walks of this route are all short and easily done, even by out-of-condition walkers.

The history of the island mirrors that of the adjacent mainland. It was held successively by the Dalriada Scots from Northern Ireland, the Vikings and finally the Scottish crown. Robert the Bruce stayed here briefly in 1307, before leaving with his small band to continue the struggle for Scottish independence which finally came about seven years later at Bannockburn.

OVERNIGHT POINTS – **Lagg** is a charming inn with palm trees and a tea garden in a wooded ravine just west of the tiny village of Kilmory. **Lamlash** is a village on the shores of Lamlash Bay, which is associated with the naval battle of Largs against the Norwegians in 1263. The 300m bulk of Holy Island lies across the bay. **Brodick**, the largest village, lies on one side of Brodick Bay, with a handsome view of the mountains to the north. Brodick Castle is across the bay, 1½ miles from Brodick Pier. Formerly the home of the Duchess of Montrose, it is now open to the public (National Trust). The castle contains a fine collection of silver, ivory and porcelain. The Castle gardens are especially notable, one of the finest in Scotland. The greater part is woodland in which rhododendrons of all kinds and colours bloom. Nearby is the Arran Nature Centre, containing displays of the island's geology and wild life. It also has a bookstore and reference library. There is a small museum in the village. **Corrie/Sannox:** Corrie is a small village of closely packed white-washed cottages, and is the hill-walking and climbing centre of Arran. Sannox is a cluster of houses a mile north, on sandy Sannox Bay. **Lochranza** is a scattered pastoral community around the shores of Loch Ranza, where the ruins of a sixteenth-century castle stand on a sand spit in the middle of the loch.

1 LAGG INN (KILMORY)–LAMLASH
11 miles (18km) 850ft (260m) OS 69

This is mainly a forest walk over the south end of the island through immature conifers, with views of the Firth of Clyde and the Irish Sea. Most of the way is on a good forest road and there is little path-finding. It is a nice leg-stretcher, quiet and deserted, with time for contemplation. We were lured ½ mile off the main route at Aucheleffan by a signpost to its stone circle, four modest standing stones in a heather clearing. The sight was not very impressive, hardly worth the mile-long digression.

The Holy Isle

NORTH – From the Lagg Inn (Inn of the Hollow), follow the A841 E for ¼ mile to the first L turn, on to a narrow paved road. Where this road turns R in ¼ mile, continue straight ahead on an unpaved farm road, passing to the W of a church. Before the road dips to cross the Kilmory Burn, you should sight farm buildings straight ahead (N) at the top of a rise. This is your first objective and your route will continue through the farmyard to a very rough farm road going N. This becomes a track bordered by trees with farmland on either side, before entering a forest. As it enters the forest the way is choked by gorse for 300yd, requiring patience and profanity to negotiate. It then turns into a fair track partly overhung with waist-high heather until the small farm clearing of Aucheleffan is reached. From here a good forest road carries you all the way to the Ross near Lamlash. Just

beyond the farm on the L the way to the stone circle is signposted. Further on your way, the farm of Auchdreoch will be seen to the R and the forest road that passes to the E of the farm joins the route. Here a sign encouragingly points L to Whiting and Lamlash. Beyond there are several side paths, the first to a chambered cairn, Carn Ban (the White Cairn), the second to Urie Loch, the third to Glenashdale Waterfall and the fourth to Whiting Bay. The forest road reaches the Ross ¼ mile from the A841 and 1¼ miles from Lamlash.

SOUTH – Leave Lamlash town centre and walk S on the A841 to the road up the Monamore Glen (the Ross). Go up ¼ mile and enter the forest road signposted 'Whiting Bay' and 'Kilmory'. Follow this road all the way to Aucheleffan. Just before Auchdreoch there is a fork, the path to the L being a faint track entering farmland with the main track turning sharp R. At Aucheleffan go through the farmyard. The forest road simply stops and you continue S over a small burn on to an old track through forest, eventually entering farmland and ending at the A841 ¼ mile from Lagg Inn (to the R). From Aucheleffan the track is fairly straight and almost due S.

high and dry

2 LAMLASH–BRODICK
4½ miles (7km) 500ft (150m) OS 69

Goat Fell from Brodick

An easy short walk over farm roads and a coastal path, offering views of Holy Island and the Firth of Clyde with its busy traffic. There are the ruins of an Iron Age fort to puzzle over (not much visible). The walk can be combined with the Lagg–Lamlash section for a long day's walk or, if done on its own, one can use the extra time to take in the small nature museum or the castle at Brodick with its exceptional gardens (the castle is about 1 mile further round the bay from the pier). This short walk we tucked into our itinerary on our departure day, a small extra treat we purchased by rising early in Lamlash so as to walk to the pier from which the mainland boat leaves Brodick. We look back on it with a poignant twinge for it seemed as we walked reluctantly towards the harbour that all Creation conspired through sight and sound and smell to give us the Isle of Arran in her most seductive garb. Truly we felt the French proverb: 'Partir c'est mourir un peu'.

NORTH – From Lamlash Pier go NE on the coastal road for 1 mile to a signpost to Dunn Fionn (the White Fort), Corrygills and Clauchlands Point. Turn L up a driveway towards the house called Prospect Hill. The driveway leads past the house to a little faded sign saying 'Dunn Fionn'. Straight ahead is a well-worn path which goes along a burn and very soon turns R to cross the burn to come out on a meadow. Here you will see a stone wall that goes N, then right-angles E and again N. Head for its NE corner and you'll be overlooking the Firth of Clyde with Holy Island looming close offshore and, if the day is clear, the mainland shimmering in the distance. Follow the wall N, heading between the hill of Dunn Fionn to the R (the remains of the Iron Age fort are barely discernible but worth the short digression, if just to sit on the ruins and daydream) and the Clauchlands Hills to the L. The path leads down towards a farm but it is blocked by a fence running E–W, bordering a forest of young evergreens. Follow the fence E until the trees thin out and then cross the fence and make straight for the farmhouse. (If you cross the fence earlier, as we did, you'll have to fight your way through prickly trees and very deep heather.) Go through the farm gate by the house and follow the track N. This track becomes a metalled road after ½ mile. It is lined with trees and a hedge, a lovely lane on a sunny day. This carries down to the A841 just 300yd from Brodick Pier.

SOUTH – From Brodick Pier take the A841 towards Lamlash. In about 300yd turn L on another paved road. In ½ mile this becomes a track, ending at a farmhouse (shown as South Corrygills on the map) in another ½ mile. Go through the gate and head S, crossing a fence in 150yd, and going W uphill along this fence until you strike a path heading S. This path takes you between the hill of Dunn Fionn on the L and the Clauchland Hills on the R. The path continues S and soon follows a wall until the latter turns sharply W. From here head SW for the far end of the wall, then across a burn and down its W side to a house and a driveway down to the coastal road. Lamlash is 1 mile to the R.

primrose

3 BRODICK–CORRIE
11 miles (17½km) 1400ft (430m) OS 69

N from Goat Fell

This walk penetrates the heart of the magnificent Arran mountains, moving up the long Glen Rosa to a high saddle and then down through Glen Sannox and back to the coast. There are spectacular views of the ridges and peaks which line both sides of the two glens. These views are ever-present but ever-changing as you move along. The more venturesome can climb Goat Fell en route with not much increase in distance but with considerably more effort. The footing is good to poor and little path-finding is required.

NORTH – Leave Brodick Pier and walk W on the A841 to the String Road (B880). Go up this to the first road on the R 1 mile from the pier, where a sign points to the cart track to Glen Rosa. Follow this road to the track which follows the Rosa Burn. Ahead is the sharp peak of Beinn Nuis. The track degenerates into a path and you will soon pass over a grassy mound, an old terminal moraine, above which to the R is the rocky spike of the 12m Pinnacle. At 3½ miles (from the pier), the glen and the path turn N, with the glen now dominated by Cir Mhor ahead. You soon cross a wooden bridge over a tributary of the Rosa Burn. There is now a long trudge, some of it boggy, up the glen to the saddle between Cir Mhor and North Goat Fell, at 6½ miles. Here you may go R and climb North Goat Fell (810m) and either return to the saddle or take one of several other mountain paths down to Corrie or Sannox. If you are going to be venturesome and take another path, we recommend Meek's book (see Further Reading page 186). From North Goat Fell we found even the Cioch na h-Oighe path not too difficult; the route to Goat Fell and down the lower part of the Corrie Burn easy going; and the upper part of the Corrie Burn (where there is no path) so delightful we actually scampered down it. But these scrambles were all done in ideal weather, so we prefer that you listen to a wiser head than ours before you go beyond North Goat

Fell. Now, assuming that you are back on the saddle, the beginning of the way down into Glen Sannox is slightly tricky, especially in mist. If you are at the point where the Glen Rosa path comes up to the saddle, go NW slanting down the N slope until a scree is reached. Go down the scree to a narrow gully (known as a whin dyke). Here some care is needed in descending its short length. Once descended, the trail picks its way down to the floor of Glen Sannox. This glen seems to us more interesting than Glen Rosa and is considerably shorter. Take either side of the burn – there are paths (sometimes disappearing) on both banks. In a dry spell we found the nearly-dry bed of the upper part of the burn to be a fine path. It can be extremely hot going in either glen on a clear windless spring or summer day and there are pools in the burns into which overheated engines can be plunged. The Sannox path passes the remains of an old barite mine near Sannox, with that whitish mineral much in evidence. The walk reaches the coastal road just at the tiny village of Sannox, with Corrie a mile S along the coast.

SOUTH – Leave Corrie or Sannox and walk N on the A841. A few hundred yards before the road bridge over the Sannox Burn there is a paved road to the L, signposted 'To Glen Sannox'. This road passes a small cemetery (interesting to tombstone enthusiasts) and becomes a cart track which carries on to the ruins of a barite mine. From here the most used way is at first by the S bank of the burn but later either side seems equally good – or bad. At the head of the glen a path up the steep slope to the saddle can be seen and the burn is left behind. The path becomes very steep, travelling a narrow gully (known as a whin dyke), just below the saddle. Here you should take care not to dislodge stones (or yourself) onto other walkers' heads (not dangerous except to the very careless). From the saddle, the well-worn path down into Glen Rosa is easily found and the way is not nearly so steep, being straightforward and passing down the W side of the Rosa Burn to the String Road and L to Brodick.

4 CORRIE–LOCHRANZA
8 miles (13km) 900ft (270m) OS 69

eider duck

A seashore and moorland route to the north end of the island, this walk affords a leisurely study of the shore birdlife – oyster-catchers, eider ducks, mergansers and other seabirds as well as the shore feeders like plover and sandpipers. The track leads 4½ miles along the shore past a jumble of house-sized fallen rocks to an isolated farmhouse, then uphill to moorland and a gradual descent to Lochranza, with handsome views of the northern hills. The walk is more spectacular coming from the north. As you move up along the hillside above Lochranza, your eyes are taken up with the view of the mountains to the south. The line of the Cir Mhor ridge clearly shows the cleft of the famed Witch's Step. As you move eastward your attention is drawn seaward, to be rewarded by a breathtaking view from the high point of land where the track curves around under a cliff to descend to the coast. Small wonder that for our Scots son-in-law this bit marked his final capitulation to the lure of hill-walking. It is amusing how he chose to let us know of his conversion. Raised in Edinburgh in a family that did not go in for outdoor activities but sharing that intense pride of the countryside that all Scots seem to have (even those separated by an ocean and a generation or two of time), he had not previously experienced much countryside walking. Married into an American family of avid walkers, he good-naturedly went along with what seemed to him an excessive expenditure of physical effort coupled with unnecessary discomfort. This resulted in much joking which firmly established him in this role. Walking with us in Arran, he volunteered to lead this section and write it up for us. It wasn't until we returned to the States and were going over our raw material that we came across his written words. They were to the effect that heretofore he had just been going along with his crazy American relatives but now he was hooked and he walked because he loved it.

158

NORTH – From Corrie walk 1 mile N on the A841 to Sannox and cross the Sannox Burn, either on the concrete stepping stones or, if these are under water, by a bridge 50yd further up. Walk back to the shore and go N for ¾ mile to the North Sannox Burn, which may be crossed on rough stepping stones or by a bridge 200yd upstream. On the far side, go through the car park past a signpost 'Fallen Rocks', over a stile to a forest road. A second stile at the end of the road brings you to the Fallen Rocks and a path leads among them and out to a pleasant open walk along the coast, past Millstone Point to a white farmhouse at Laggan. Here, turn L and go along the N side of the farmhouse directly uphill until the old cart track to Lochranza is reached. The track slants upward NW across the slope and is difficult to see, being mostly visible by the cuts into the hillside. The way grows steadily more discernible and soon becomes easy to follow, staying parallel to the shore but high above it for about a mile. You finally swing W over a boggy plateau, to drop down to a farm road in Glen Chalmadale. This reaches a paved road going past a golf course and on to the A841 at the S end of Lochranza. The pier is 1 mile to the R. The few establishments offering accommodation are scattered mostly along the motor road.

SOUTH – From the pier walk SE along the A841. In about 1 mile from the pier, a signpost indicating footpaths to Laggan, Cock of Arran, etc leads you L across the Chalmadale Burn, then R along an ascending farm road. In ½ mile a weathered sign points L off the farm road to a track to Laggan and the Cock. Follow this track up and over to the shore at Laggan. (You will pass a track going L to the Cock, too faint to lead you astray.) Your track first gently ascends the N slope of Glen Chalmadale, crosses a plateau and then descends SE a bit more steeply across a hill slope facing the Firth, to the shore at Laggan, where the way is S along the shore to Sannox and Corrie.

oystercatcher

159

MULL WALK Islands
40½ miles (65½km)

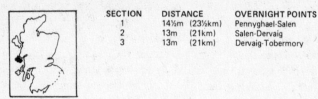

SECTION	DISTANCE	OVERNIGHT POINTS
1	14½m (23½km)	Pennyghael-Salen
2	13m (21km)	Salen-Dervaig
3	13m (21km)	Dervaig-Tobermory

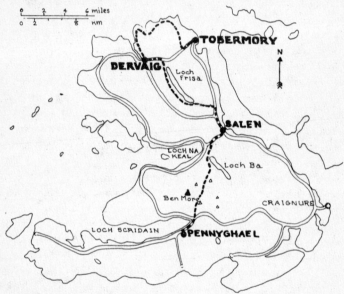

ACCOMMODATION (OM&L)
(except as noted below, overnight points have
more than 2 hotels)

Pennyghael: Kinloch Hotel, 1 B&B
Dervaig: Bellacroy Hotel, Drumnacroish
Hotel, B&Bs

PUBLIC TRANSPORT (H&I)
buses from Craignure, ferry Craignure-Oban, train Oban-Glasgow
(Mon-Sat)

In this Walk you explore the island of Mull. Unlike Arran, which is a compact lozenge-shaped drop in the sea, Mull is an untidy splatter, its perimeter much indented. The settlements are few, widely spaced and, except for Tobermory and Salen, limited in accommodation. We have traced a large S-shaped route, going from the south shore of Loch Scridain, through the island's mountains to the small coastal village of Salen, thence by Loch Frisa, Mull's largest inland loch, to Dervaig, a tiny eighteenth-century village, and round the high, twisting northern coast to Tobermory, the island's best-known and most populous place.

Mull suffered great loss of people during the callous Clearances, much of it unnecessary. As you walk over its beautiful isolated ways, you should keep in mind that this now inhospitable terrain once sustained hundreds of crofters. Efforts are being made to bring back the fertility of the land and increase economic opportunities. The largest single landowner is the Forestry Commission, its activity changing the landscape in many places.

OVERNIGHT POINTS – **Pennyghael** is a tiny hamlet of a few houses scattered from the Kinloch Hotel (the Post Office) to the road going south to Carsaig. From the hotel, two day-long walks of exceptional interest are available for the more leisurely; one to the Nun's Cave west of Carsaig, the other to Lochbuie east of Carsaig. **Salen** (the salty place) is a harbour village on the Sound of Mull. Although most of the buildings were built about 1800, the site is one of great antiquity. 1½ miles north of Salen is Aros Castle, a medieval fortress of the Lords of the Isles. This consortium of seventeen clans under MacDonald of Islay always presented difficulties for the Scottish Crown. **Dervaig** (little grove) is a village with enough charm to delight the most exacting traveller. Kilmore Church, standing at the crossroads in a grove of trees, has a pencil steeple, unusual in Scotland. The village street is lined with low white-washed houses built in pairs (1799). Each house came with a garden and grazing rights on common hill land. Two attractions within walking distance are the Mull Little Theatre and the Old Byre, a museum of early life on Mull. **Tobermory** (Well of Mary) is a colourful town which lines the bowl-shaped harbour and climbs the hills around it. There was a small Christian settlement here from early times but the present town was established in 1789 by the British Society for Encouraging Fisheries. Unfortunately, fishing never prospered here. The waters of the bay hide a sunken ship from the Spanish Armada, its treasure still unrecovered.

1 PENNYGHAEL–SALEN
14½ miles (23½km) 1080ft (330m) OS 48

This is a fine walk, going by way of an old hill track from the head of Loch Scridain by Loch Ba to Salen on the Sound of Mull. It is a good sample of Mull's mountainous south. Ben More (966m) is much in evidence during the walk. The track climbs past its striking east face, a 700m sheer wall plunging to the floor of a valley. The way is easily followed, the footing good.

We were fortunate to see deer on the slope, not because this area has a small deer population but because the deer are so wary and have such keen noses and ears as well as an uncanny sense of intruders. This means that generally they have moved off before you are in good viewing range. They also make seasonal movements within their home range, high in summer and low in winter, so the time of year affects your chances of seeing them as does the weather. This gives you an inkling why stalking is an art and why your presence on the hills in the stalking season is so unwelcome.

If you see a herd, take time to sit quietly and study it (binoculars are useful here). There are two kinds of herds, hind herds and stag herds, and they move about separately except during the 2½-month rutting season in the autumn. The hind herds, made up not only of the hinds and their calves but also of young males up to 3 years old, are larger and they pre-empt the best grazing. The stag herd includes only the older stags. Which kind of herd is before you is quickly ascertained, since the stags will all be antlered. There are other, more subtle differences, worth a longer observation. In the hind herd, the older the hind the more wary she is, so those who are most aware of your presence and who do not go back to grazing after being alerted are apt to be the older, wiser hinds, with one in particular being the leader. When moving off, the herd will follow this leader. If a younger one gives the alarm (a short loud bark), the leader will come over and take command. The whole herd responds to an alarm by standing perfectly still, forefeet together and heads raised. If you remain motionless and the wind is right, they may gradually go back to grazing. The leader will be the last to do so and will continue to be alert. When they do move off in alarm, it is as a body with the leader in front. If she stops they stop and none will go in front of her. The stag herds, on the other hand, behave quite differently. They seem unable to warn each other, no leader takes charge, and each stag decides for himself as to when and where he runs.

NORTH – Leave the Kinloch Hotel at the head of Loch Scridain (the hotel is also the PO of Pennyghael, although the OS map shows Pennyghael as being on the road to Carsaig 2 miles away) and walk N on the A849 across the flat valley of the Coladoir river for 2¾ miles. Just beyond an old disused bridge (marked Teanga Brideig on the map) is a sign 'Loch Ba, Loch na Keal and Clachaig, 8 miles'. From here a hill track leads up the N side of the narrow Sleibhte-coire valley to a col between Creag Mhic Fhionnlaidh and Torr na h-Uamha. Looking back, you get a good view of the strath you have left and ahead you see the magnificent E face of Ben More at the head of Glen Clachaig. The track zig-zags N down the W slope of Cruachan Dearg to the floor of Glen Clachaig, fords the River Clachaig and joins another track on the S shore of Loch Ba (Loch of the Cattle). Go W along Loch Ba for 2 miles to the tiny village of Knock on the B8035. Walk N and E along the B8035. Loch na Keal (Loch of the Cells) will be on your L across the River Ba. In ¾ mile a sign points R to the mausoleum of Major-General Macquarie, the Ulva-born 'Father of Australia'. Salen is ahead, 3½ miles from Knock.

SOUTH – At Knock a track L off the B8035 is signposted 'Loch Ba, Glen Clachaig and Loch Scridain'. At the col at the head of Glen Clachaig, you have the choice of two routes. The track down the Sleibhte-coire goes L. The other, more interesting, track (difficult to find coming N) goes R over another saddle just N of the modest top of Guibean Uluvailt. Beyond the saddle, the track disappears but you can easily pick your way across the wide, grassy S slope of Beinn nan Gobhar down to either the A849 or the B8035. This alternative provides good views of Loch Scridain and the strath at its head. The original track came down to Ardvergnish Farm and from there it crossed the tidal flats at the head of Loch Scridain by a ford ending at the Kinloch Hotel (shown on the OS map). Walkers should not attempt this ford without obtaining local advice.

red deer

2 SALEN–DERVAIG
13 miles (21km) 530ft (162m) OS 47

Salen, old pier

This walk is moderately strenuous, stretching from Salen on Mull's east coast to Dervaig which sits by a finger of seawater on its north coast. It combines forest rides with open moors and pastures and there are constant views of lochs, hills and distant mountains. It is a fine introduction to Mull's hilly north and the way is easy to find. There is one trackless section but it parallels Loch Frisa, which affords ample guidance. The footing is fair to excellent.

There are two attractions near Dervaig which deserve special mention. If possible try to include one or both of them in your stay. The first is the Mull Little Theatre – this theatre is the creation of Barrie and Marianne Hesketh, a talented husband-and-wife acting team who perform to the highest professional standard. They are a company of two so their repertory is exclusively those plays for two players such as *The Fourposter* by Jan de Hartog. The theatre itself is a converted barn which has only forty intimate seats to offer, so reservations are a must. To reach the theatre, walk south from the church on the road to Salen. The turnoff is at the cluster of A-frame wooden chalets on the left-hand side of the road. The second attraction is 'The Old Byre'. It is 1 mile from Dervaig on the Calgary road, and is a small museum with a well-done audio-visual presentation using two re-created croft settings. It tries to give a picture of the contrasting life between that of the black houses at the time of the Clearances and that of the small crofter after the Crofting Act had given him relative security. It succeeds in pointing up the suffering of the savage Clearances. As you walk over this land that used to produce a living for so many and see how it has reverted to heather and bracken with even the sheep (for whom the land was cleared) in short supply, you can ponder on man's shortsightedness as well as his inhumanity.

NORTH – From the Craig Hotel in Salen go N on the A848. Just before the turnoff to Glen Aros is the Dal na Sassunach (field of the stranger) to the L where the Mull and Morvern Agricultural Show has been held since 1832. The name is said to come from the murder of an Englishman by MacArthur, head of a famous piping school on Ulva, in a jealous rage over the former's perfect piping. On the headland to the R is the ruined Aros Castle, once the stronghold of the Lord of the Isles. Continue on the A848 and in about 1 mile from the bridge over the Aros river go L on a forest road (the second you will pass, 2½ miles from Salen). Go W to Ledmore (5 miles) (we visited a silver workshop here in 1980) and cross the Ledmore river to Tenga Farm. Here go N on a track through fields and pastures. The track soon disappears. Head NW for the SW (L) slope of the small hill of Cnoc nan Dubh Leitire. (We were not able to spot the standing stones marked on the OS map ¾ mile NW of Tenga.) Beyond the hill, walk parallel to Loch Frisa and about ¼ mile above it, to a gate and track through a plantation (the gate is easily seen as you come across the farmland). Follow this track high above Loch Frisa through the forest and across open land to Achnadrish Farm (a B&B in 1980) (11½ miles) and the B8073. Go L uphill on this winding road to Dervaig 1½ miles away, taking advantage of the short cuts that walkers have made across its switch-backs. At the summit there are good views ahead to Dervaig, its sea loch and valley and views back to Loch Frisa. On a clear day the hills of the Outer Hebrides can be seen. Just below the summit, 200yd R, inside a forest fence, is a stone circle.

SOUTH – Walk E on the B8073 from Dervaig to Achnadrish Farm and go R through the farmyard to a track SE. Beyond the plantation head across the SW slope of Cnoc nan Dubh Leitire (no track) and across farmland to Tenga Farm. Go L on a farm track to Ledmore and R to the forest road going S and SE to the A848. The mountains seen ahead during much of the walk are those on Mull's SE, with Dun da Ghaoithe (766m) the highest. Ben More (966m) can be seen occasionally to the S.

gorse

3 DERVAIG–TOBERMORY
13 miles (21km) 490ft (150m) OS 47

Dervaig

This is a delightfully varied walk along country roads, forest rides and hill tracks round Mull's NW coast, with sweeping views of the sea, featuring Coll and Tiree to the west, Ardnamurchan to the north and the Cuillin Hills of Skye in the far distant northwest. The way is easily followed but does require close attention to its twists and turns. The footing is good to excellent.

EAST – Go NW from Dervaig village on the paved road along the NE side of Loch a Chumhainn to its end at Cuin (1 mile). Here you pick up the unpaved estate road of Quinish and go N, avoiding a number of L forks. Beyond the Home Farm the way becomes a farm track. Shortly after the track leaves a wooded section you will see, 100yd off the track to the L, a standing stone on a green plateau, the stones's 3m height a striking landmark. At Mingary (3¼ miles) the farm track stops and a path circles E and then SE, becoming a forest road in ½ mile. At the first crossroads go L, first in forest and then in the open, for 1 mile and then L again, running NW past Ballimeanoch along the edge of another forest. If you wish to see what a crofting community of 140 years ago looked like, at 558440 take the L fork for 300yd to a faint track L. You will see the ruins of half a dozen small houses ahead. They are soon explored. One seems better built than its neighbours. Here must have lived 30 or 40 people, to be scattered abroad by the Clearances. How difficult for us to visualise their life, tending to see only the remains of relative material poverty and not the close-knit warmth of a stable small community. Take the next R fork, enter a forest and fork R again in 300yd. This track carries you to the Glengorm estate road at Sorne (6¾ miles). Go R on this road for 100yd and then go L downhill through a gate to a farm road leading past a croft on your L. It turns into a grassy track which enters a forest and climbs up to join a forest road coming up from the R. (There is a small sign saying 'Forest walk' at this junction). Continue straight ahead on this forest road which circles round the headland of Ardmore Bay. You will have views of the water until the road turns SE and the forest cuts off your view. You will soon emerge from the forest and go along its E edge until you join the Glengorm estate road again. Turn L down this road to the B8073 and go L to the A848. Go L a short distance into Tobermory town centre.

WEST – From the waterfront in Tobermory walk S on the A848 to the Dervaig road (B8073). Go R for ½ mile to the Glengorm estate road. Follow this road until just before it enters a forest and take a track going R along the forest edge and into the forest. When the route forks, take the L fork. Suddenly you will catch sight of Ardmore Bay below and, as you proceed, you will get expanding views until you are walking in the clear, with the forest rising above you on the L and dropping sharply to the sea on your R. As you round one bend Glengorm Castle appears ahead, the only vertical shape above the rounded mounds of green forest. Where the forest road takes a decided turn L downhill, you will leave it (sign 'Forest walk' at this point) by a grassy track going to the estate road at Sorne. Go R 100yd to a farm track going L beside a plantation. It soon enters the forest and joins another forest road. Go L through open land and forest about 1 mile to the second road on the R. Take this across the Mingary Burn to a lesser-used crossing track and go R. This track enters a mixed forest and soon becomes a path which leads you into the open, with fine views of the surrounding countryside, the sea and offshore islands. Continue on this path to Mingary where a farm road goes S to the Quinish estate road to Dervaig.

Glengorm castle

NOTES

Note A Public Transport and Accommodation

In our walking we have found it difficult, even when living in Scotland, to find out what is available by way of both public transport and accommodation for the out-of-the-way places in which you will be walking. The following notes may therefore be helpful to you.

Public Transport

The Walks have each been selected so that the start and finish both have public transport facilities available. With very few exceptions, the other overnight points can also be reached by public transport. For each overnight point, the type of public transport available and its nearest connection to Scotland's major transport network are given on the pages which introduce the Walk. Occasionally the frequency and time of service is noted. The name (abbreviated) of the source of more detailed information is also given, full names and addresses being listed at the end of this Note. You may therefore make your own inquiries directly to these sources. You may also obtain details on the type of current service and its schedule by (a) inquiry at Scottish Tourist Board Information Centres, or (b) by inquiry at the larger airports, train and bus stations, and ferry offices as you are en route to a Walk. For the Walks in the Highlands and Islands, the single most useful book on public transport facilities is the *Highlands and Islands Comprehensive Transport Timetable* (available from the Highlands and Islands Development ment Board, Bridge House, Bank Street, Inverness, or from the larger Tourist Information Centres). This covers 50 of our approximately 90 overnight points, including all the Walks in the Northwest Highlands and most of the Walks in the Grampians. It is small enough to carry easily and is reasonably priced (80p in 1980). An equivalent for the Southern Uplands is the *Borders Travel Guide*, which covers travel to all the overnight points in the Tweeddale and Borders Walks (available from the Borders Regional Council (30p in 1980), see address at end of this Note). For Postbus timetables, write to the Scottish Postal Board, 102 West Port, Edinburgh EH3 9HS, or inquire at the local post office (a good idea in any event).

Accommodation

If you stay on the beaten tourist track in any country, a call to your travel agent will usually suffice. However, in our Walks you will be well away from the tourist paths (this is one of the charms) and only a very few of the overnight points have accommodation listed with travel agents. Thus, that easy solution is effectively denied you. Here is a distillation of our experience and what we've gathered from tourist departments, innkeepers and fellow travellers.

1. BASICS

(a) Start finding out what is available and make reservations well in advance of your trip – perhaps one month if you live in Britain and at least two months if you live abroad.

(b) We feel it is an absolute must that you have *confirmed reservations before you set out.* You are not the casual car traveller that you may have been before, easily able to cover many miles in search of lodgings (and in Scotland the car traveller lacking accommodation may well have to do that in the summer). Many of our overnight points have a limited number of beds, making it especially likely that they will be fully booked.

(c) To secure confirmed reservations you must finally verify on both sides the date(s) and the kind of accommodation required; and send a deposit if requested.

(d) When you have made a firm commitment for a certain date, it is assumed that, even if you are not able to use the accommodation, you will honour all the associated costs unless these are waived. Where a deposit has been paid this is considered sufficient to meet such costs. Where a deposit has not been required, more important than any legal obligation is the moral one of keeping your word. If we sound preachy, forgive us, but most of the inns and all the B&Bs are not part of an impersonal hotel chain but very small businesses on which the owners often depend for their livelihood. In any event if illness or weather has halted you in your tracks, let your innkeeper or landlady know you will not be arriving.

2. FINDING WHAT IS POTENTIALLY AVAILABLE

With the basics firmly in mind, you now need a list of what is potentially available and some idea of prices. Unfortunately, there is no single complete listing for all of Scotland, still largely a land of local initiative. The Scottish Tourist Board publishes two annual volumes on *Where to Stay in Scotland*, one for hotels and guest-houses and the other for B&Bs (available at a charge from the Scottish Tourist Board, 23 Ravelston Terrace, Edinburgh EH4 3EU). Although these list over 3000 places, they probably miss half of the potentially available ones and miss entirely those for many of the more remote overnight points.

However, other accommodation registers are available from the new electoral regions and from tourist organisations.

On the pages which introduce each Walk we have included information on available accommodation for the overnight points. It is entitled 'Accommodation', is only listed where limited and gives the names of hotels and guest-houses where two or less are available (as far as we were able to find out – the list may not be complete). It also indicates where there are two or fewer B&Bs but does not attempt to list them as they can change rapidly. If the overnight point is not listed it does not mean that no accommodation is available, but rather that there are more than three hotels or guest-houses. To find a lodging, you can contact the tourist organisation which has the most complete list. This is given in abbreviated form next to the heading 'Accommodation'. The full names and addresses for these abbreviations are given at the end of this Note. In a remote area, where all else fails to uncover a bed for us we have found a letter to the local postmaster (with a SAE) sometimes works.

3. MAKING A RESERVATION FROM A DISTANCE

The most positive way to secure a reservation is to write directly to the accommodation source. You should make a specific request, rather than a tentative inquiry, stating the date of your arrival, length of stay, your number, the type of accommodation required, and asking what deposit is required. For the smaller establishments a self-addressed and stamped envelope is a must. If you live abroad, you can enclose an International Reply Coupon, purchased at any post office, in lieu of a British stamp. You might also ask the addressee of your correspondence to pass on your request to another establishment in the event that they themselves are fully booked.

A few organisations maintaining accommodation registers now offer an advance booking service by mail – ideal for the walker. (Those offering this service will note it in their register.) The service is only for places within the area served by the particular organisation and there is normally a charge (in 1980 approximately £1). The bookings are provisional and you must confirm or reject the reservation directly with the establishment concerned, generally within five days of notification of the provisional booking. Tayside Regional Council is the only organisation offering a *free* accommodation reservation service and only within their region. They will accept your request by letter, telex or telephone, obtain a tentative reservation at the desired lodging (or an equivalent one in the event of a full booking), and post you an answer within 48 hours. If you do not have time to write for the

Accommodation Register, Tayside have indicated that they would be willing to work with only a general idea of the type of accommodation desired plus your itinerary. Such services stress item (d) under Basics.

Two other tourist services may offer some help to you once you are in Scotland. First, all Information Centres will attempt to secure accommodation for you within their local area, if you call in person at the particular Centre. The radius of a local area is roughly one of our day's walks so you cannot normally reserve very far ahead. Second, for distances beyond the local area, the Scottish Tourist Board's Book-a-Bed-Ahead Scheme may help you but again, you must go in person to one of the Information Centres offering that service. Both these schemes guarantee a firm booking. You pay a deposit, deductible from your bill at the end of your stay, plus a standard charge for communication and service (50p for the local service, £1 for the Book-a-Bed-Ahead Scheme in 1980). These services are of somewhat limited usefulness to the walker since they require appearing in person and since so few of the route points have Information Centres (only about 1 in 5 have the Centres and not all the Centres have the extended service). It does help that you will probably enter Scotland through Prestwick, Glasgow or Edinburgh, all of which have Tourist Information Centres providing *both* services.

One of the overnight points requires the use of a Youth Hostel, it being the *only* source of accommodation (Alltbeithe on the Glenshiel Walk, see page 114). Nineteen of the other overnight points also have Youth Hostels (noted in the Index against the overnight point). These hostels are open to anyone holding a membership card issued by one of the 50 countries within the International Youth Hostel Federation, including Scotland. Advanced booking is recommended in busy periods. For more information write to the Scottish Youth Hostel Association, 7 Glebe Crescent, Stirling FK8 2JA.

Names and Addresses of Tourist Organisations

Arran — Arran Tourist Organisation,
The Pier, Brodick, Isle of Arran

Bord — Department of Planning and Development – Tourism Division, Borders Regional Council, Newton St Boswells

Cent — Central Regional Council,
Viewforth, Stirling FK8 2ET

Edin — Tourist Information and Accommodation Service,
9 Cockburn Street, Edinburgh EH1 1BQ

D&C — Dunoon and Cowal Tourist Organisation,
Pier Esplanade, Dunoon PA23 7HL

D&G	Dumfries and Galloway Tourist Organisation, Douglas House, Newton Stewart
Ft Will	Fort William, Lochaber and District Tourist Organisation, Fort William
Gramp	Department of Leisure, Recreation and Tourism, Grampian Regional Council, Woodhill House, Ashgrove Road West, Aberdeen AB9 2LU
K&C	Ask for *Kyle and Carrick District Council Accommodation Guide* from Strathclyde (Strath)
O&M	Oban, Mull and District Tourist Organisation, Argyll Square, Oban
Spey	Spey Valley Tourist Organisation, Main Road, Aviemore
Strath	Department of Leisure and Recreation, Strathclyde Regional Council, Viceroy House, India Street, Glasgow G2 4PS
Suth	Sutherland Tourist Organisation, The Square, Dornoch
Tay	Accommodation Reservation Service, Tayside Regional Council, 26–28 Crichton Street, Dundee DD1 3RD
W. Ross	Wester Ross Tourist Organisation, Gairloch IV21 2DN

Names and Addresses of Public Transport Operators

WSMT	Western S.M.T., Nursery Avenue, Kilmarnock KA1 3JD
WAS	W. Alexander & Sons, Guild Street Bus Station, Aberdeen
Bord	Borders Regional Council, Newton St Boswells

Note B   Route Finding

We have chosen our routes and written our route information keeping in mind people who may never have walked on anything other than clearly marked and well-defined paths. Because our routes are rarely signposted or blazed and because the way is often indistinct, a minimum knowledge of the use of maps and compasses is desirable. If you can read a car map, can follow instructions in cookery recipes, and can take a few minutes to make friends with a compass, you can gain this minimum knowledge from our Basic Lesson (see below). For those who wish to be able to cut the apron strings of this guidebook, we add material (Slightly Advanced Lesson) that will help you gain the skill to move across any unmarked terrain with the aid of only map and compass.

1. Basic Lesson

The three tools you will be using are the guidebook, maps and a compass. For most of our routes only the first two are necessary, but on occasion you will need the compass in order to distinguish approximate directions relative to north.

a MAPS AND MAP-READING

The maps we recommend are the new Ordnance Survey 1:50,000 (1¼in to the mile or 2cm per kilometre. Do not let this large number put you off – it simply means that 1in on the map equals 50,000in on the ground. The mapmakers can find no better way to say it.) You may have the older OS 1in maps (1:63,360 scale or 1in to the mile). These are no longer sold (except for a few special areas) but are perfectly adequate to use if you have them. The scale of either of these map types is a nice balance between the walker's need for detail and for economy of load (the 1:25,000 scale OS 'walker's' maps are good for small areas but would necessitate up to four times the number of maps per walk and are not available for all our routes). Assuming that everyone is familiar with road maps in this car age, the OS maps will be strange only in their symbols and their use of contour lines to show elevations above sea level. You will pick up the meanings of most of the map symbols through encountering them as you go along. Their meaning is given on the right-hand or bottom edges of each map. Walkers, of course, are most interested in the footpaths (single-dashed black lines) and unsurfaced minor roads (double-dashed black lines). *Dotted* black lines are *not* footpaths but electoral boundaries (civil parish or equivalent), a confusion we once fell into. The contour lines are not needed for this basic training. If you are interested, see our Slightly Advanced Lesson below.

The terrain features mentioned in the text correspond to those on the new OS maps (the spelling may be slightly different on the older OS maps) or to familiar topographical features. A glossary of the Gaelic map features, their pronunciation and English meaning is given on page 187. A short glossary of common features is given here for the benefit of those to whom the words may be unfamiliar.

Aqueduct A large pipe carrying water from a reservoir, either for hydroelectric power or for urban use.

Bothy A hut, now often kept in repair as shelter for walkers and climbers.

Burn A stream or creek.

Col or Saddle The highest point on a pass, bealach or larig and generally a low point on the hill ridge or mountain range.

Deer fence A high wire fence to keep deer out of newly planted forests.

Glen A valley.

Gorge A narrow valley with steep or vertical sides.

Pass, Bealach or Larig (Lairig) The easiest way over a hill ridge or mountain range and, therefore, used by ancient and modern man alike.

Ridge The top of a range of hills or mountains.

Shieling A summer hut, occupied temporarily by person watching over grazing animals, now generally in ruins.

Stile A step or series of steps going over a fence or wall.

Shoulder A side of a hill or mountain.

In spate Referring to streams and rivers, when unusually high water occurs from heavy rains. May be dangerous to cross at such times. (See Safety page 182).

INTRODUCTION TO THE COMPASS

Types of compass There is a wide variety of compasses on the market and a similar range of prices. *Any* compass is adequate. However, we recommend a fluid-damped compass, in which the needle moves in a clear liquid, as an un-damped needle will quiver annoyingly when hand-held. Compasses come with additional features such as a luminous dial for use at night, a protractor base to aid direct use on a map, a sighting device for more accurately determining the bearing of a distant object, and several methods of carrying (wrist strap, neck cord). They all add to the weight and price. We feel the most useful additional feature is the protractor base. If you want this aid, the least expensive one sold for orienteering will be quite good enough.

Reading the compass Compasses are almost all marked in *points* and *degrees* (a few engineering compasses are in degrees only, a few old marine compasses in compass points only). The compass points used are the four familiar ones: north, east, south and west (N, E, S, W) and the four intermediate points of NE, SE, SW and NW (the old mariners among us will be swift to mention that there are 32 points in all, an education we can easily forgo). The compass circle is also

174

divided into 360 degrees. Most compasses are marked every 2°, with actual values shown every 20°. You will need to know only the eight points mentioned.

The working part of the compass is the magnetic *needle*, which will point towards magnetic north. For your purposes you can assume this to be the same as true north (the small differences are discussed in the more advanced lesson). Almost always the *north* end of the needle is dark-coloured, usually red. It is best to check this with another compass before you set out.

The following are simple steps that will help you master your compass.

1 To find north, hold the compass flat and steady and away from iron and steel objects. If the compass is held near an iron object such as a pocket knife or belt buckle it may be deflected from north during that time. It can be checked by holding it at several distances from your body just to see if the reading changes. The needle's dark end should point in the same direction regardless of how you rotate the case or how near your body you hold it.

2 To align the case, rotate it until the needle points to the N on the case. If *you also* face the direction the needle is pointing, you will be facing *north*.

3 If you want to find a particular direction other than north – for example, northwest – do not rotate the case but keep the needle of the compass on N and move only your body around the compass until you are looking over the centre of the needle and directly facing the NW mark or 315°.

4 If you want to walk towards the northwest, do not walk *and* watch the compass. Instead, point your body towards the northwest, then carefully pick out a prominent landmark at some distance along this direction. Once spotted, walk towards it. Stop and check your direction from time to time. This is the essence of moving by compass. Simple, isn't it!

C ROUTE-KEEPING

Before you set out open your guidebook for the day's walk, then select and open out the proper OS map(s). Read the section description and find and follow it on the map, familiarising yourself with the general characteristics of the way. When you pack up your belongings, keep your book, map(s) and compass handy. You are now nearly ready to start out. Before you do so, however, one further chore is recommended. Try to work our how long the expedition is likely to take. Do this by using your own personal version of what is called the

Naismith formula (after the gentleman who first proposed it). The original formula was to divide by 3 the distance in miles that you expected to walk (that is, you were assumed to walk at a base rate of 3mph) and add to that calculated time an additional ½hr for every 1000ft of height to be gained. This translates into the metric system by dividing the distance in kilometres by 5 and adding 1.6hr for every 1000m of height gained. This is fairly fast walking these days and 2–2½mph plus 1hr for every 1000ft of height gained may suit the more sedentary walker. This translates into the metric system as 3¼–4kph plus one-third of an hour for every 100m height gained. At the beginning of each of our one-day walks the distance and height gained are noted both in the English and metric units. Choose your formula, make your calculations and hope you are not too late for supper.

Most of the one-day walks require only a map and the guidebook, with the compass not really needed. However, where the way grows indistinct or disappears, the compass comes into its own and the three work together. Where the route skirts a loch or follows a burn or river, the preferred bank to follow will be given as a compass bearing, such as 'the SW shore', 'the N bank'. Sometimes you will be going over a piece of high land, following one streambed up and one down. There must then be a stretch with no watercourse to follow and here the route description will give a compass direction to follow between the two streams. It will also name and describe the land to go over (often as a pass between two easily seen peaks).

One important caveat – ALWAYS BELIEVE YOUR COMPASS. Even experts occasionally become disoriented on sunless days and swear their compasses have gone wrong. It is easy to get turned around in your sense of direction, especially if you lose sight of known landmarks. Don't panic, just get out your trusty compass and map and get re-oriented.

2 Slightly Advanced Lesson
We hasten to state that true competence in moving over wild country does not come out of books. However, for those who may be interested in increasing their ability beyond what we have considered the basic requirements, the following few notes may be useful.

a COMPASS NORTH AND MAP NORTH
Except at a few places on the earth, the compass does not point true north, but towards magnetic north. The difference between the two is called the *magnetic variation*. To make matters more complicated, the

vertical lines on the OS maps are not generally aligned exactly with true north. These lines are called *grid north*. You can, however, ignore the difference between grid north and true north because the OS maps do not give the magnetic variation for the particular location but do give the difference between grid north and magnetic north (a composite of the magnetic variation and the difference between true and grid north, which you can now forget). The actual values of the difference between magnetic and grid north, given on each map, range for Scotland between 7½° West to 8½° West in 1976, *decreasing* about ½° in 5 years, thus ranging from 7° to 8° West in 1981. For the small amount of track-less work you will be doing on our routes, you can ignore these complexities and still connect up with the next section of the Walk. However, it is more fun to be accurate and the little picture on the OS maps in the note on NORTH POINTS is the best way to explain whether to add or subtract the difference in order to convert a compass bearing to a grid bearing or vice versa. One practice taught in orienteering which will help in this is to pencil in lines on the map about 1 inch apart parallel to the magnetic north–south alignment. Then you can lay your compass on the map and turn the map until these pencilled lines are parallel to the magnetic needle. This is a fast and fool-proof method.

b MAP READING

The contour lines on the map are intended to display the terrain relief; that is, to show how the land humps up. These lines are easy to understand but difficult to use. They are lines joining points on the earth's surface that are at the same elevation above sea level. Somewhat confusingly, on the first issue of the new OS maps (1:50,000), their height above sea level, printed occasionally along the contour lines, is in *metres* but their vertical interval, the incremental height between two adjacent lines, may be 50 *feet*. This is because the contour lines of the first set of 1:50,000 maps were drawn from the older 1in maps, which used that vertical interval. We should mention that the elevations of the various peaks and summits are given here and in the 1:50,000 series maps in metres also. Now to explain how to use the contour lines. A moment's reflection will make you realise that when the lines are shown close together, the land is steep, and when far apart, it is relatively flat. Be very careful to spot places where the contour lines disappear altogether. This is not because the Ordnance Survey has become fed up with drawing them – it can't, the terrain has become perpendicular! Avoid such places like the plague. Our routes do not go near them and if you find yourself in their vicinity

177

you are not only a trifle lost, you may be in danger.

The problem is to visualise the actual earth surface from the map representation. Some people seem born with this ability, most are not. Everyone, however, can learn quite a bit by comparing the map and the land while travelling along. Armchair travelling doesn't seem to help much – we are constantly surprised by the 'seen' terrain as compared to the terrain visualised just studying the map. But once in the field, comparing real and map features makes the contour lines come alive.

C ROUTE-KEEPING

You are now ready to navigate across charted but unmarked country. You had best start with a day's walk whose track is reasonably clear underfoot, so you can practise. Here the problem is one of finding where you are *along* the track by compass bearings taken on real terrain features that are also on the map. You must know one of two things: either the identification of the real features (the names they go by on the map) or your position on the track. If you don't know either, the problem is insoluble. So you must start at the beginning of the track, when you do know where you are. Sit down and open the map and hold it flat (folding the unrequired portions reduces its unwieldiness). Take the compass and orient the map so that map north points to true north (if you have forgotten the last session on the compass, just align the map grid with the compass needle). Keeping the map from rotating, sight by eye over your location on the map in direction lines along which prominent real features can be seen. Look down at the map along the same direction lines and see if you can find the feature on the map. Some idea of the approximate distance will help sort out the features along each line.

Now, if you can initially identify just a couple of features, then, as you move along the track, you can reverse the process and find out where you are on the track. This can be done by orienting the map again and, sighting on the known features (whose bearings now will have changed, since you have moved. They also may look a little different, since you will see them from another aspect, so keep an eye on them in between sightings). Try to visualise where you would have to be standing along the track to obtain these new bearings. This can be done more precisely by taking the *reverse* of the compass bearings (easiest to work in degrees and add or subtract 180°, whichever gives you a non-negative answer) and, positioning the compass on the landmark, see where the reverse bearing would cut the track. It sounds complicated but you should find it easy in practice. Now, new features will come into view as you move along and these should be identified before the old features disappear from sight. These new features will, in turn, help you find your location along the route. The trick is not to lose sight of old landmarks before you pick up new ones.

In case all this is making you nervous, the way will frequently cross streams, pass lochs, and go by houses or their ruins, that need no compass work to identify and which will place you quite precisely on the map. Also the routes we have chosen are those used by other people in other times to get most easily from one point to another. Reasonably, they went around mountains rather than over them, around bogs rather than through them. The routes travel valleys, go over low passes, hug streambeds – anywhere the gradient is easiest, the footing the driest. Thus when the track grows indistinct underfoot, a knowledge of the general direction of travel and an eye on the terrain will help you move along, much as the first traveller did. This is the essence of being route-wise – the integration of a few clues from map, compass and the terrain (plus a few from us) and a natural tendency towards economy of effort, into confident and easy travel along indistinct and intermittently seen tracks.

A word on carrying the map. Besides folding the map into a convenient size for easy use, it is wise to make or invest in a transparent map case to keep the map dry. A heavy-duty plastic envelope or even a folded and taped sheet of medium-thick transparent material (0.1mm or so) will do. It should be big enough for the folded map to show a substantial portion of the route and its surrounding features. We find the OS maps seem to fold and fit most readily into a 25cm by 30cm (10in by 12in) case. This will display at least half a day's walk and the terrain out to about 5 miles on each side of the route. Unfortunately, it is an awkward size to stow or hang on the pack, will blow around if hung on a cord around your neck, and is altogether a nuisance if you want it handy for frequent consultation. You can be inventive here.

One final sophistication in map usage that is used sparingly here is a six-digit number to denote a spot on the OS map not otherwise identifiable. When this number is encountered the best explanation of it is given on the right-hand side of every map under 'INCIDENCE OF ADJOINING SHEETS AND NATIONAL GRID REFERENCE SYSTEMS'. We avoid its use whenever possible, meaning (unfortunately), that it is important as a landmark when it *is* mentioned. With a little practice you should soon find it quite easy.

And last, a word on getting lost in mist. Finding your way in mist is the most difficult feat in route-keeping. It is also a bit unsettling and, very infrequently, can be dangerous. When there is thick mist at your overnight point, at breakfast time or at your starting point as you set out, you sensibly should wait until it lifts. But when the base of the clouds only just covers one of the high passes, it is hardly dangerous to venture up since your distance in the mist will be short and you can retreat if you feel it necessary. However, if you are well into the back country and the mist suddenly clamps down, there is the possibility of it being present for some time and your being forced to move through it. Here are some recommendations if this should occur:

(1) Don't panic – your worst enemy is fear of the mist and not the mist itself.

(2) Sit down and wait a bit (in a sheltered spot, of course). Mists are generally mercurial beasts and can come and go rapidly.

(3) While you sit, consult your three best friends: your compass, map and this guidebook. Is going forward or backward the quickest way to lose altitude and thus perhaps get below the mist? Which route direction is better marked (cairned, posted, painted or visibly trodden)? Which way has the widest safe swath of ground to fumble one's way by compass? Is there a stream that can be followed to safety?

(4) If you do decide to move, keep to the path if possible and go slowly. If the way is cairned or posted, move from cairn to cairn or post to post. Two people help here – one going ahead to find the next post or cairn, the other to stand lonely by the last one as a point of reference. Do not go out of voice or whistle range in this search (this is why a whistle is often carried).

(5) If you must strike off without benefit of track, cairn or post, use your companion as a landmark by sending him or her ahead along the desired compass heading until he or she is just visible, stopping there until you come up. Repeat the process until clear of the mist. To find the desired compass heading, if you know your present location roughly and the location of where you want to move to, the compass can be used as a protractor, ie a device for measuring angles. The orienteering compass with a movable bezel and a long, straight side is easiest to use. Lay the long edge on the map so that it points from your present location to the desired point. Rotate the movable bezel until the lines on it point to grid north. The desired grid direction can now be read from the degree mark on the movable bezel that is over the mark on the fixed bezel (the bezels being the rings around the compass needle). With a little more difficulty the cheapest compass can also be used. Place the compass on the map over your present position so that the North mark points in the direction of the new location. Keeping the compass firmly on the map, rotate both until the needle is aligned to grid north. Read the bearing under the compass needle and subtract

it from 360°. This is the desired grid direction. You will remember from our earlier remarks on grid and magnetic directions how to get the magnetic direction you will be using. A last word of comfort is that if all the foregoing complicated instructions fly out of your head, our routes are such that you can work to the nearest magnetic cardinal point (N, NE, E, etc) to the direction you want to go and still get safely to civilisation. Exact headings will be vital only if you venture on to the mountain tops and these our routes assiduously avoid.

Note C   Countryside Manners

In brief, countryside manners are simply the Golden Rule applied to the particular circumstances of the countryside. You are sharing the environment with many others – land owners, the Forestry Commission, the National Trust, and other walkers, for example – and you should be sensitive to their rights and needs. Many of us are also coming to believe that the environment itself has rights. A provocative thought.

The following list is offered to remind you of the specifics of good countryside manners:

● Respect private property and keep to paths when going through estates and farmland. Where possible, avoid climbing over walls and fences and replace wall stones you might dislodge. CLOSE ALL GATES THAT YOU OPEN. This is easy to forget when your party is of any size, as the gate opener walks on and the last person through may not be aware that it was initially closed. This is best avoided by having the one who opens it stand by to close it.

● Do not leave litter. You might, on occasion, carry out others' litter.

● Be careful not to disturb sheep in the lambing season (March–May).

● Avoid deer-stalking and grouse-shooting country during the stalking and shooting season (usually August–October, but inquire locally).

● Keep dogs under control, on a leash when requested, especially during the lambing season.

● In forests keep to the paths, avoid smoking and do not light fires. Avoid damaging trees in newly planted forests.

● Safeguard water supplies.

● Protect wildlife and wild plants.

Note D Safety

The traditional classification of hillwalkers is amblers, ramblers, scramblers and danglers. Under this classification, our Walks are nearly all in the rambler class, with scrambling extremely rare. In addition, the Walks remain at fairly low altitudes, generally below 1500ft (460m). There is a small likelihood, therefore, of high winds, low temperatures, and mists, compared to ventures to the hilltops and mountain peaks. Thus the Walks are relatively safe – much less dangerous than hill climbing or even walking along a busy highway.

Having said all that, it must be added that there are two unlikely but possible dangers that may occur during our Walks and commonsense actions to be taken in their event. These dangers are hypothermia and incapacitating illness or injury.

Hypothermia is a dangerous lowering of one's body temperature through some combination of low temperature, high wind and poor clothing. The symptoms are incoherent speech, confusion of thought and diminished ability to walk, perhaps leading to occasional falls. The person affected will usually not know that he or she is suffering from it. Prevention is simple – adequate clothing. The remedy is also simple – a hot beverage and a bit of high-energy food (sugar or chocolate, for example). If the condition is mild, restoration to normal is immediate. We stress again that hypothermia is most unlikely at the low altitudes of our Walks and vanishingly so with proper clothing. Final insurance is a walking companion and a thermos of hot tea, coffee or cocoa.

We cannot envisage any injury more serious than a turned ankle and, of course, walkers are never ill. However, if you worry about the possibility of becoming incapacitated on the Walk, you should do one or both of two things – take a companion who can go for help, or inform someone, such as your next night's host, to call for help if you do not appear by an agreed hour. Help will come from trained volunteers of the local Mountain Rescue group, reached through the police (dial 999). In the unlikely event that someone in the party is too ill or injured to move and a member goes for help, it is important to note the map location of the immobile member in order to help the rescuers find him. Most exact would be the six-digit grid number (see Route-Keeping page 179) which locates a point to 100m. If not, the nearest landmark and the distance and direction from it would help. Not only does it aid the rescuers, it can speed up the rescue immensely as an exact location may aid in bringing in a helicopter to the site. If you have asked to have help sent in the event of your non-appearance at the expected time, BE SURE TO CALL OFF THE HELP IF IT IS NOT NEEDED

– for example, if you turn back or simply do not go in the first place. To raise a false alarm and put many people to unnecessary inconvenience is surely a grievous crime among walkers.

Finally, you may be tempted to climb a mountain or two during your walk. If so, you should know your basic Mountain Code. On the higher tops it is possible to get Arctic conditions at any time during the year – high winds, low temperatures, snow, ice and poor visibility. Therefore, before you climb: you should already know how to use map and compass, know the weather signs and local forecast and plan within your capabilities; know simple first aid and the symptoms of exposure; and know the mountain distress signals. When you go, never go alone; leave written word of your route and report on your return; take windproofs, woollens and a survival bag; take map, compass, torch and food; wear climbing boots; and keep alert. If there is snow or ice on your route always take an ice axe and climbing rope and know how to use them; and learn to recognise dangerous snow slopes. And if your only introduction to mountaineering is these foregoing words – don't go!

One additional source of possible danger is in fording streams, especially when in spate, ie when greatly swollen by rain. The most general rule is to move upstream until the stream grows sufficiently shallow (as you pass more and more tributaries) to cross with ease. When and where you do finally cross, before you do so, remove your boots, socks and any lower clothing that might get wet (no place for prudery here), put socks and clothing in your rucksack and put the boots back on (wading a rocky streambed in bare feet is just asking for trouble). If in company, link arms, with less muscular members sandwiched between the stronger, and wade across, preferably facing downstream (easier to catch yourself if you stumble). Once across, after a dance of thanksgiving to warm the lower extremities, pour the water out of your boots, resume your clothing, your equanimity and your walk.

Note E   Access to Land in Scotland

In going on to privately owned land in Scotland, while you cannot be arrested for trespass you have no legal right to enter without permission of the owners except where a public right of way exists. You may be asked to leave and can be forcibly evicted if you refuse. You can only be prosecuted, however, if you cause damage to the land, its livestock or buildings. These are the legalities. In practice the attitude of most landowners is one of neutrality. If your countryside manners are impeccable, it is not likely that your access will be thwarted (see Countryside Manners, page 181).

Prohibitions are more likely to emanate from organisations like the Ministry of Defence or the Royal Society for the Protection of Birds rather than from private landlords (we know of no such prohibitions on any of our Walks as of 1981). Public authorities are usually most cooperative. The Forestry Commission, while warning of the dangers of starting fires, provides and encourages the use of attractive forest walks and picnic sites. The National Trust for Scotland allows virtually unrestricted access to their land, as does the Nature Conservancy to nature reserves.

During the late summer and early autumn, deer shooting may be in progress on the Scottish hills crossed by some of our Walks. Notices asking walkers to 'Keep Out' may be posted. This should not be a serious problem on any of our Walks which, by and large, keep to defined tracks. However, if you do see any such notices inquire locally about exactly where the shooting is taking place and, if necessary, ask for advice about alternative routes.

For a number of our Walks, the way has been used by the public without let or hindrance over a prescriptive twenty years and, under Scots law, there is a public right of way. But, since some of the rights of way are being challenged by some landowners and we do not wish to involve the holiday walker in controversy, we do not indicate where a right of way is held to exist. We recommend that you consider your presence in the countryside a privilege rather than a right. You may wish to support the work done by the Scottish Right of Way Society in keeping open rights of way. For information write to the Honorary Secretary, 28 Rutland Square, Edinburgh EH1 2BW.

Note F   The Types of Way
You will be on a variety of ways, from paved roads (when unavoidably necessary) to trackless ways. A number of general types of way will be used in the descriptions of the Walks. Some idea of their genesis and nature will be useful to you. They are listed below in order of ease in following them.

Paved roads (tarmac, ashphalt, concrete) – There is not much to say here except to deplore the need to walk on them occasionally. Walk on the *right* facing traffic. Where there is no verge or shoulder to walk on, you will share the macadam with vehicles. Walk defensively.

Carriage roads – These are the roads which preceded the paved roads, built in the nineteenth century for carriage traffic. Most were incorporated into the motor-road system but a few were not. You will not encounter them often. They will be level, dry and their way easily in evidence, even though now disused.

LRT – This stands for Land Rover Tracks. These are unpaved private estate roads negotiable by four-wheel-drive vehicles. Reasonably good walking and, of course, easily followed. They are proliferating, and many will not be on your map.

Military roads – The Highlands were essentially a roadless area as late as 1725. In that year the British government began construction of a series of military roads, first connecting the various garrisons built to control the clans in that turbulent region and then extended. By 1767, some thousand miles were constructed. They are generally associated with General Wade, who constructed the first 250 miles. While some were incorporated into later roads, many were abandoned. It is on these latter you will, on occasion, find yourself. Their course is frequently obscured and their footing is good to poor.

Roman roads – In Scotland, Roman roads will be encountered only below the Clyde–Forth line. The roads are typically a series of straight sections and, even where overgrown, easy to follow.

Tracks – The most primitive of the ways made for wheeled vehicles, many dating from the medieval period. The term is now also being applied to unpaved roads through forest plantations (forest tracks).

Rides – Open swaths left in forest plantations, partly as firebreaks, partly for access. They may be overgrown with scrub, contain paths in various stages of usefulness or have unpaved roads (forest tracks).

Paths – These form the bulk of the way in this book. The upland habitations were confined to the more fertile valleys, especially those accessible by sea lochs or near the shores of the larger freshwater lochs. As there was some commerce between these habitations, footpaths came into existence. Many must have been in use for thousands of years. While the early travellers kept away from the bogs and hill tops, they took the shortest route between two points and so, because of the steep gradients, these routes were only infrequently incorporated into the later roads. You will occasionally be on more recently made paths such as those of the Forestry Commission and National Trust. They will vary in their visibility from clearly defined paths to faint and intermittent tracks over reasonably good ground.

Drove roads – The Scottish cash crop was their black cattle, driven each year down to the lowlands or to England for sale. The roads over which they moved were simply the more gentle and less boggy terrain. They are today about as the drovers found them, mostly trackless swaths a little better for walking than the surrounding country.

Trackless ways – Infrequently, you will be faced with crossing country with no visible way. This is a pleasant challenge to most of us. The section material will give you compass headings, landmarks and distances. You will need the map and compass, especially in poor visibility. If you are new to finding your way by these aids, see Route-Finding, page 172. Common sense, knowing which end of the compass points north, and some self-confidence are all that are really needed. If you feel that you may be anxious in walking over a trackless section, bypass that day's walk or choose another route not having any trackless bits. A walk need not be an exercise in bravery. However, for most, crossing a trackless area will be fun and will engender a real sense of achievement.

Note G   Further Reading

Darling, F. F. & Boyd, J. M., *The Highlands and Islands* (Glasgow 1977)

Feachem, R., *Guide to Prehistoric Scotland* (1977)

Fitter, R. & A., *The Wildflowers of Britain and Northern Europe* (1978)

Hunter, T. H., *A Guide to the West Highland Way* (1979)

Haldane, A. R. B., *The Drove Roads of Scotland* (Newton Abbot 1973)

MacInnes, H., *West Highland Walks* (2 vols) (1979)

Macnab, P. A., *The Isle of Mull* (Newton Abbot 1970)

Meek, R. L., *Hill-Walking in Arran* (Arran 1975)

Moir, D. G., *Scottish Hill Tracks* (2 vols) (Edinburgh 1977)

Nethersole-Thompson, D., *Highland Birds* (Inverness 1977)

Perry, R., *Highland Wildlife* (1974)

Peterson, R. et al, *A Field Guide to the Birds of Britain and Europe* (1971)

Poucher, W. A., *The Scottish Peaks* (1974)

Price, R., *Highland Landforms* (Inverness 1976)

Scottish Mountaineering Trust, *Scottish Mountaineering Club District Guide Books* (8 vols)

Scottish Tourist Board, *Angler's Guide to Scottish Waters* (Edinburgh); *Scotland for Hillwalking* (Edinburgh); *Walks and Trails in Scotland* (Edinburgh)

Taylor, W., *The Military Roads of Scotland* (Newton Abbot 1976)

Note H Glossary of Gaelic Words frequently encountered in Ordnance Survey Maps

From *Place Names on Maps of Scotland and Wales*, Ordnance Survey, 1973. Suggested pronunciations are from *Illustrated Road Book of Scotland*, Automobile Association, 1971.

aber	mouth or confluence of a river
abhainn	(pron. av'uin) river, usually *avon*
allt	(pron. alt) brook, burn, stream
ard, aird	a high point, promontory
ban	white, fair
beag	(pron. bak) little, small
bealach	(pron. byall'-ach) breach, pass, gap
beinn	(pron. byān) a mountain, conventional form *ben*
binnean	small and peaked mountain
bo, plural ba	cow, cows
both, bothan	primitive house, bothy
buidhe	(pron. boo'-i) yellow, golden coloured
caisteal	castle
ceann	(pron. kyenn) head, headland, usually *kin, ken*
clach	(pron. klach) a stone, *clachan*, stones, hamlet
cleuch, cleugh	(pron. kluff) ravine
coire	(pron. kor'-e) a cauldron, kettle, circular hollow, other form *corrie*
col	depression in a mountain chain
cruach	(pron. kroo'-ach) stack, heap, haunch
dearg	(pron. jerrack) red
druim	the back, ridge. Usually *drem, drom, drum*
dubh	(pron. doo) black, dark
dun	(pron. doon) a fort, castle
easg	(pron. ask) bog, fen, natural ditch
eilean	(pron. el'an) an island
gleann	(pron. glyan') narrow valley, dale, dell
inbhir	(pron. in'-ver) confluence, place at the meeting of river and sea, other forms: *inver, aber*
lairig	a pass
leathan	(pron. lya-un) broad
loch	a lake, arm of the sea
lochan	small loch
maol	(pron. mull) headland, bald top, cape
meadhan	(pron. me'-un) middle, central

meall	(pron. myal) knob, lump, rounded hill
monadh	(pron. mon'a) moor, heath, hill, mountain
mor	great, large, tall
mue	(pron. moocht) a sow, pig
ob	a bay, creek, haven
obhar	(pron. o'-ur) dapple, drab, dun-coloured, sallow
ord	a round, steep or conical hill
poll	(pron. poul) a pool, pond, pit
riabhach	(pron. rĕ'-ach) drab, greyish, brindled, grizzled
rubha	(pron. roo'a) promontory, cap
sean	(pron. shen) old, aged, ancient
sgeir	(pron. skeir) a sea rock, skerry
sgorr, sgurr	(pron. skor, skoor) a peak, conical sharp rock
strath	(pron. stra) a valley, plain, strath
stob	(pron. stop) a point
suidhe	(pron. sooi'-ge) sitting, resting place
taigh, tigh	(pron. ty) a house
tir	(pron. tyēr) country, region, land
tir-nan-og	the land of the ever young
uaine	(pron. ooin'e) green
uamh	(pron. oo'av) a cave, a grave

please close!

INDEX

Names in italics indicate overnight points on walks. YH indicates a Youth Hostel at an overnight point; YH(3) indicates its distance from an overnight point. Page numbers in italics indicate illustrations.